21 July 96
To Mari...
Thanks for the memorable
visit — much love
carolina, SEAN & David

P.S. AND Marilyn —
thanks for the memorable
genes!

Feminist Parenting

Struggles, Triumphs & Comic Interludes

Edited by Dena Taylor

The Crossing Press
Freedom, CA 95019

Also by Dena Taylor

Red Flower: Rethinking Menstruation

co-editor with Amber Coverdale Sumrall:

Women of the 14th Moon: Writings on Menopause
Sexual Harassment: Women Speak Out
The Time of Our Lives: Women Write on Sex after 40

Photo Credits
Judith Arcana by Pauline Kochanski
Ardena Shankar by Dianne Glidden
Penelope Sky by Helene Constant © 1994

Library of Congress Cataloging-in-Publication Data

Feminist parenting: struggles, triumphs & comic interludes/ edited
    by Dena Taylor.
        p.   cm.
    ISBN 0-89594-690-4 (pbk.)
    1. Parenting—United States. 2. Feminism—United States. 3. Sex role—United
States. I. Taylor, Dena.
HQ755.8.F45   1994
649'.1—dc20
                                                                94-21275
                                                                CIP

Editor and publisher gratefully acknowledge permission to reprint the following:

"Essay" by Alta is reprinted from *The Shameless Hussy: selected stories, essays and poetry* (The Crossing Press, 1980), with author's permission.

"The Book of Daniel" by Judith Arcana is adapted from *Every Mother's Son* (The Women's Press, London, 1992) with author's permission.

"Baptism" by Ellen Bass is reprinted from *Our Stunning Harvest* (New Society Publishers, 1985) with author's permission.

"The Age of Reason," copyright 1981 by Mary Kay Blakely, is reprinted from *The New York Times*, March 26, 1981, with author's permission.

"Life Excerpts" by Naomi Feigelson Chase is excerpted from a forthcoming novel of the same name. Printed with author's permission.

"Challenges" by Jean Ellis is an excerpt from "To Great Applause" in *Alone Together* edited by Jenny Morris (The Women's Press, London, 1992). Reprinted with Ellis's permission.

"The Grandmother Network" by Elena Featherston is excerpted from her book *Skin Deep* (The Crossing Press, 1994) with author's permission.

"Matthew at Thirteen" first appeared in the *Minnesota Review* (Spring 1979), then in *Romance and Capitalism at the Movies* (Cambridge: Alice James Books, 1985) and is reprinted with author's permission.

"Reflections of a Feminist Mom" by Jeannine Ouellette Howitz originally appeared in *On The Issues* (Fall 1993). Reprinted with permission of Howitz and *On The Issues*.

"The Proper Roles" by Adair Lara was originally published with a different title in *The San Francisco Chronicle*, July 25, 1991. Reprinted with author's permission.

"Man Child: A Black Lesbian Feminist's Response" by Audre Lorde was previously published in a longer version in *Sister Outsider* (Crossing Press, 1984). Reprinted with publisher's permission.

"Boy Thangs" by Kate Luna is adapted from her show "True Kid," performed on stage. Printed with author's permission.

"Lesbianism and Judaism" by E.L. Moore was originally published in *Tiferet*, Oberlin College, Ohio, October 1991. Reprinted with author's permission.

"Raising Sons" by Robin Morgan is reprinted with author's permission from Ms., November/December 1993, copyright 1993 by Robin Morgan.

"Toys Are Us" is an excerpt from *Growing Up Free: Raising Your Child in the '80s* by Letty Cottin Pogrebin (McGraw Hill, 1980). Reprinted with author's permission.

"The Intolerable Burden of Loss," copyright 1993 by Minnie Bruce Pratt, originally appeared as "One Good Mother to Another" in *The Progressive*, November 22, 1993. Reprinted with author's permission.

"What about the Boys?" by Anna Quindlen is reprinted from *The New York Times*, May 2, 1993, with author's permission.

"To Lilith" by Lynn Saul was originally published by the Jewish Women's Resource Center in New York in their *Lilith Chapbook*, 1991. Reprinted with author's permission.

"Guys and Dolls" by Jean Tepperman was originally published in a slightly different form in the *San Francisco Bay Guardian*, January 5, 1994. Reprinted with author's permission.

"Cinderella's Sisters" by Barbara Unger has appeared in *Inside the Wind* (Linwood, 1986) and in *Wordsmith*. Reprinted with author's permission

*To my parents Anne and Martin Taylor
and my daughters Becky and Anna Taylor*

Table of Contents

Introduction

Feminist parenting, as I have come to think of it, means raising children outside of the traditional male-female roles, in which the females are disadvantaged and the males are in a privileged position. It means raising girls and boys to challenge the discrimination and exclusion of women when they see it. It means raising kids to grow up wanting to change the status of women in society. It means raising boys to speak out when they hear other boys making sexist remarks, and to see girls as friends and equals. It means raising girls to be free to make their own decisions about sexuality, marriage, and having children, and it means freeing boys from the pressure to be macho. It means being a feminist yourself. And in its broadest sense, it means raising children to be humanists and environmentalists.

Some of the parents writing for this collection were themselves parented in a feminist way. Most were not, however, and chose to bring up their children differently than they themselves had been. This choice of navigating unfamiliar territory calls for creativity, flexibility, honesty, hard thinking, and humor.

As you will see, some ideas worked and some didn't. Often there is great pressure from the outside world—school, friends, other family members, religion, TV, movies—which undermines the work of feminist parenting. Some parents won't give their daughters Barbie dolls; some purposefully buy dolls but not guns for their sons. One mother takes her son shopping in the girls' department because the colors are brighter; another takes her daughter to the boys' department because the clothes are sturdier. They empower their daughters, sensitize their sons. They change the wording of the books they read aloud to their young children, and they teach both daughters and sons to look critically at the media.

Most of the accounts in this book are by mothers, with three pieces by men and three by daughters. I wish there were more by fathers and by children raised as feminists, but the reality is that most feminist parents are mothers, and I simply didn't receive many submissions from children.

There are pieces here by heterosexual and lesbian parents, partnered and single, disabled and able-bodied. They are racially, economically, and geographically diverse. Some of the stories made me laugh out loud; others brought tears.

Not having sons myself, I was touched by the lengths to which some mothers went to instill in their sons a feminist consciousness, and how these sons in turn taught their mothers to truly like men. Many mothers of sons spend a lot of time "in the ear" of these sons educating them about our sexist world.

This is not a how-to book. It's a book of stories by people who are trying to make a difference in their own lives, the lives of their children and, by extension, the community and the world. It is a book that shows the ways that some parents are bringing a feminist consciousness into their childrearing. And in a few cases, how some children (usually daughters) have enlightened their parents about feminism.

I wish to thank all who sent in work for this book, whether it was included or not. By the volume of pieces I received, as well as the many letters saying how important it is to write on this subject, I realize that feminist parenting is of passionate concern not only to me, but to many others.

In parenting, we shape the future. By raising our children in a feminist way—from the small everyday interactions to the harder, more demanding things we do—we are making the world a more equitable place.

—Dena Taylor
Santa Cruz, May 1994

The Proper Roles

"At this point in history, we cannot rear our children in a world free of sexism. But we can try our best to rear free children at the same time as we work to change the world."

—Letty Cottin Pogrebin,
Growing Up Free

Essay

Alta

one hesitates to bring a child into this world without fixing it up a little. paint a special room. stop sexism. learn how to love. vow to do it better than it was done when you were a baby. vow to make, if necessary, new mistakes. vow to be awake for the birth. to believe in joy even in the midst of unbearable pain.

to bear a child. to bare oneself to that experience. to touch a being with love that hasnt done a damn thing to earn your love. to learn how to love. to care for when it cant take care of you when you're sick. to step out of yourself & learn to step back into yourself. this is the second step, the one we, as women, are just learning. to love without giving oneself away. to stand up without being sat back down.

to watch how the children do it, & to let them love us. to realize ourselves in a reciprocal world.

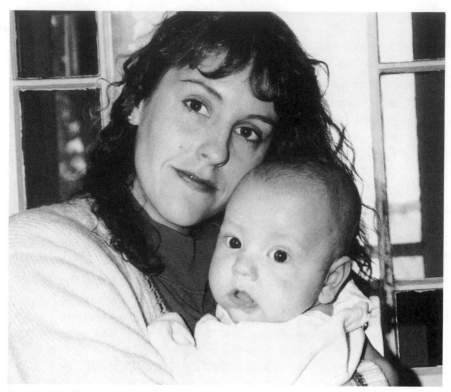

Jeannine Ouellette Howitz and son.

Reflections of a Feminist Mom

Jeannine Ouellette Howitz

I am seven months pregnant, slithering along my kitchen floor. The ruler I clutch is for retrieving small objects lost in the dust jungle beneath my refrigerator. After several swipes I come up with a pile of dirt and a petrified saltine, so I get serious and press my cheek against the floor, positioning my left eye just inches from the target zone. I spot it—the letter "G," a red plastic refrigerator magnet. "Here it is!" I cry, hoisting myself up to offer this hard-won prize to Sophie, my momentarily maniacal toddler. Her face collapses into a sob as she shrieks, "NOT THAT ONE!"

Sophie is 22 months old, and in the final stages of potty training, which I remember as I feel a gush of warm and wet on my outstretched leg. Wet clothes bring more tears (hers, not mine), and I quickly strip off her clothes, then pull off my own with one hand while I slice and peel an apple with the other. I might have barely enough time while she eats to run upstairs, grab dry clothes, and toss the dirty ones into the basket before I'm urgently missed.

That was how I came to be standing in the middle of my kitchen with the magnificence of my naked abdomen hanging low and wide on a clammy June afternoon. The sweat of my exertion had just begun trickling between my breasts when the phone rang. It was an old friend with whom I'd been out of touch for a while. I panted hello, eyeing Sophie as she climbed up and out of her booster chair to totter precariously on the table top. "What are you doing home?" my friend wanted to know. "Don't you work at all anymore?"

Don't you work at all anymore? Again and again since entering the life phase which positioned my work in the home, I have encountered the judgments, however unconscious, of those whose definition of work excludes most of what I do. The same system that discounts my labor scoffs at its rewards, which, like my productivity, are impossible to measure by conventional standards. By limiting our view to one which allows only for paid employment, usually only that located outside the home, to be included in the understood meaning of the word "work," we support the process through which all that we do and all that we are as women is ultimately devalued and despised.

Like most labels applied to women's roles, "working mother" is extremely inaccurate and defeating, because it foolishly implies that there is another type of mother: the non-working variety. Being a mother is work. On the other hand, it is equally absurd to call mothers who are not employed outside the home "full-time mothers," as this unfairly suggests that employed mothers are only mothers part-time. Ridiculous as they are, these labels go largely unchallenged, even by many feminists. They are a sinister trap, imprisoning women in feelings of inadequacy about whatever roles we have chosen or been required to perform.

The same process that forces a woman to say "I don't work" when she performs 12 to 16 hours of unpaid labor every single day at home ultimately transforms most female-dominated professions into mere chores that women and men alike come to consider less desirable and important than other types of work. Once stamped with the kiss of death "women's work," we can forget entitlement to the same respect and fair wages a man would get for equivalent labor.

Before motherhood, I sold advertising at a newspaper, with hopes of working my way into editorial. However, my sales performance exceeded standards, and I was quickly promoted to a well-paying position in management which required me to build a classified department from the ground up. I forged ahead until my daughter was born, when, after reexamining our options, my husband and I decided one of us should stay home with her. Although he was happily working in his chosen field, John's income as a schoolteacher was half that of mine, which rendered him the financially logical choice for at-home parenthood. But it was I who jumped at the chance, albeit scary, to shift the gears of my career and of my life.

When my maternity leave was up, I told the publishers that I wouldn't be returning to the office. Surprisingly, they offered me the chance to bring my daughter to work with me. I was thrilled; those long days at home with an infant weren't exactly what I had imagined. I discovered that although I didn't always enjoy my job, I did enjoy the recognition it provided me—something I found was not a part of the package for home-working moms. While my sister spoke with unveiled envy about all the reading and writing I would now be accomplishing, in reality I was lucky if I brushed my teeth. So I took the deal.

Seven weeks old on her first day at work, Sophie fascinated the staff as only a newborn can. A two-minute trip to the copier often turned into a half-hour social ordeal as one person after the next stopped to exclaim over her. She was a great diversion for a young and predominantly single staff. I had no idea, as a new mother, how fortunate I was to have an extroverted baby. It was my own introverted nature that suffered from the constant sensory bombardment. I was uncomfortably aware of my special status, and fighting a losing battle to hide how much time it actually took to care for Sophie on the job.

In a culture where women feel guilty to call in sick to work when a child is sick, it was tremendously difficult to be in an office setting, drawing a full salary, and to say, "Sophie's crying now—this phone call, this meeting, this project, whatever it is, will have to wait." In a society that expects workers to give 150 percent dedication to the job, and considers motherhood a terrible detriment to productivity, it was incredibly stressful and even painful at times to experience such a personal conflict in a very public setting when the two worlds collided.

For six months, I toted a baby, a briefcase, and a diaper bag back and forth from home to my office, which at first housed the crib and swing, after which came the walker, the play gym, and the toy box—not to mention the breast pump equipment and mini-diaper pail. I could hardly see my desk, let alone get to it. Not that it mattered, because by that time I wasn't doing any work that required a desk. It had gotten crazy, and I knew it. The circles under my eyes and my continued weight loss told me it was time for a change.

I explored every alternative I could think of, from researching and visiting daycares to negotiating with my employers for a part-time or home-based position, or a combination of the two. However, my key position on the management team required a full-time presence in the office.

Offering my resignation was an extremely difficult decision, particularly in light of my gratitude for the progressive opportunity to have my daughter on-site. My employers and I finally agreed to view my departure as the beginning of an indefinite unpaid leave that left the door open for my possible return at some unpredictable future date.

A two-month notice allowed me to finish up the last big sales project of the quarter, while my daughter was cared for by a neighbor. I got an unforgettable taste of the superwoman syndrome, rising at 5 a.m. and dashing out the door by 6 to drop Sophie off and commute an hour to the office for a grueling nine-hour day. This was followed by a long drive in Minnesota winter rush-hour traffic to pick my daughter up and go home, and was topped off with a couple of frantic hours that my husband and I spent getting everyone fed and Sophie bathed and to bed so

9

that we could start all over again after what felt like a quick catnap. Relief overcame me as my last day at the office arrived, and I packed my diaper bags for good.

Our plans had always included my return to full-time paid employment upon our children's entry to school, which meant that, for the benefit of our financial solvency, we should have another baby quickly if at all. We chose "quickly," and shortly after our daughter's first birthday I was pregnant again.

I started stringing for our local newspaper, rushing out to city council and school board meetings as soon as my husband dragged himself through the door at seven o'clock. I got paid a measly 25 dollars a story, but since the meetings were at night and I could write the stories at home, I didn't have to pay for childcare. Moreover, it was the first time I saw my writing published; it signaled a turning point for me as I finally made the leap from advertising to editorial.

Since then, I've stuck to what I'm passionate about as I navigate the uncertain waters of these transitional years. I've redefined my priorities, and am using this time to lay the groundwork for a career that is going to work for me long after my children are grown. Like the many women who grow home businesses while growing young ones, I've discovered meaning in my personal work that was previously absent.

These days, since I do perform paid work from home, I could have an easy answer to "Don't you work at all anymore?" I could say that I am a freelance writer working at home. It's true, and since I know, based upon my own research, that it gains me a great deal more respect in the eyes of the asker than saying that I'm home with the kids, I'm tempted to offer it up. But I won't because every time I do, I'm perpetuating a system that defines work only in terms of what men have traditionally been paid to do, and discounts most of what women have traditionally done for centuries.

I have to make perfectly clear when I say that I work at home, I'm talking about the childcare and the home maintenance activities which utilize my talents as a manager, nurturer, healer, wise woman, acrobat...and retriever of small objects lost in the dust jungle beneath my refrigerator. Otherwise, people automatically dismiss these activities and conjure up a false image of an orderly day spent at the computer doing paid work. This strain toward clarity requires a lot more effort than calling myself a full-time mom, or proclaiming that I'm taking time off to be with my kids (motherhood is not a vacation), or, worst of all, concurring that no, "I really don't work at all anymore." It demands concentration and patience, but it can be done.

We must find new words, or new combinations of and meanings for old words that more accurately reflect our reality. When we don't—when we resign ourselves to the old words that apportion us less worth than we deserve because it's less awkward and just plain easier—we are validating a description of ourselves that we know to be false. This danger is like that of looking into a fun house mirror, without challenging the falsehood of the contorted stranger staring back at you. Eventually, you're going to believe what you see is you, and that twisted version of yourself becomes the only truth you know.

Inside Daddy's Lunch Box

Kathy Melin

My daddy has a gray lunch box. It is round on the top to hold his big thermos bottle. In the winter, he has hot soup. In the summer, he has lemonade with ice cubes in it.

Every morning, he takes his full lunch box and walks to work. His legs are so long that he can walk backward faster than I can run forward. Daddy comes home at 5 p.m. And then his lunch box is empty, except for the wrapping papers and a few crumbs.

Last week, he brought surprises home in his lunch box. My three brothers all got knives. They can sharpen twigs with them to roast marshmallows. They can carve animal shapes out of blocks of wood. They can throw them into the soft ground.

I got a pen and pencil set. It came in a plastic case with a clear cover. They are turquoise blue.

I can think of a lot of things to do with a knife. I could cut up an apple and eat it. I could slice pieces of paper in half and fold them into small hats for my dolls. I would keep my knife in my pocket just in case someone needed it. Anyone. And if I cut myself, I wouldn't cry.

My daddy gave all my brothers knives. They have pearly handles and sharp blades.

My brothers and I play together every day. I can swing the farthest on the rope. I'm fast at bicycle tag. When we play mountain climber, I never fall.

I asked him why I didn't get a knife, too.

He said he'd just stop bringing things home.

I'm eight. My little brother is six and a half. He got a knife.

I said, "It's not fair."

Daddy said, "But you're a girl."

"But girls can still use knives," I said.

Daddy walked away.

When Daddy came home tonight, he had a surprise in his gray lunch box. I snapped open the metal buckles. Inside were three turquoise pen and pencil sets and one knife with a pearly handle.

"Thank you, Daddy," I said.

"Uh-huh," he said.

"Thanks a lot," I said.

"You're welcome," Daddy said.

I gave him a big hug.

"Kathy," he said, "thank *you* a lot."

Toys Are Us (excerpt)

Letty Cottin Pogrebin

Unless the adults around them are open to flexible roles, children will ignore toys they fear are gender incongruous. There's not much sense in giving a doll to a little boy whose father wouldn't be caught dead rocking a baby. But if more men knew how important toys are for child development, more fathers might become less rigid for the good of their children if nothing else.

Before our daughters learned to read, I used to read game directions aloud to them, altering the inevitable male pronoun to "he or she," or, more often, "you"—as in "You should roll the dice and move clockwise on the board."

One day, after Robin could read by herself, she brought me the instructions for a game she was starting to play.

"This game isn't for girls, Mommy," she told me. "Look how it says a player should move *his* piece when *he* draws a card."

I had to explain that in gameland, as in English usage, "*He* means *you*."

I've watched our two daughters grow into adolescents without a single request for a toy gun. They've played chase games in which there are pretend fighting, horrific injuries, and melodramatic dying scenes of victims rolling down hills or falling in a heap. But there has been no shooting. When I asked them why, they said it never occurred to them to add guns to the dramas.

On the other hand, our son—raised on the same values and prohibition of toy guns—has occasionally come under the spell of a fancy toy tank or shiny revolver and attempted a feeble plea for "just one." His play sometimes has included pretend finger guns, war whoops, and "Bang, bang, you're dead." When I walked in on such a fracas, he always looked sheepish. Although I never stopped the action, David can read my mind.

Once, when he was about six or seven, he fashioned a gun-shaped object out of a piece of wood and announced that "it's a miracle gun that shoots life back into people who get dead." David reveres life. He covers his ears when someone tells a story about suffering. But he retains a definite fascination with guns. If it wasn't obvious from his dramatic play as a small child, it would be crystal-clear from the meticulously detailed drawings of artillery, bombers, and gunboats he has produced throughout his later childhood years.

Is this because he's a boy, or is it because he's seen guns everywhere defined as the accoutrements of male power and glory? We'll never know the answer until our culture tells its children that weapons are not symbols of strength but signs of weakness.

No one expects to protect children from the violence in life. However, to protect them from the glorification of violence and to deny parental *approval* of weapons as tools of power is a parent's right and obligation.

Certainly, if every toy has the potential to teach a child something, then a toy gun will teach some boys to need a real gun and to enjoy pulling the trigger. The most moral and responsible parents ask their children to accept a contradictory message: We *think crime and killing are dreadful, but here's a cute little toy rifle for Christmas.*

The name of the game is fun, and the world is full of playthings that both complement a parent's consciousness and warm a child's heart. Does your child have enough of those kinds of toys? To find out fast, use this test for nonsexist children's rooms: Could you move a six-year-old girl's toy chest into a six-year-old boy's room in confidence that he would enjoy its contents? If not, how many and which toys would you remove to make the collection more "suitable" for a boy; what toys would you add, and why?

I once watched a little boy select a flower press as a gift for his friend in such a way that it was clear he coveted the item himself. "Are you kidding?" said the boy's father. "We can't get Peter such a sissy present." Judging from the crushed look on the boy's face, I'd say his interest in preserving flowers died on the spot.

If I had to name the one play item in our house that lasted the longest and gave the most, it would have to be wooden blocks. For more than ten years our set of unpainted wooden blocks in the shapes of arches, squares, rectangles, columns, half circles, and triangles gave all three children thousands of hours of fun. We've watched the blocks be transformed into bridges, castles, space stations, zoos, highways, farms, street scenes, and split-level homes, accessorized with little rubber animals, wooden people, cars, trains and street signs. For landscaping, fresh flowers and weeds. And for mirrors and lakes, aluminum foil. Curtains, wallpaper, and murals were homemade. Other structures have been used to hide in, jump off, climb up, perform from, and balance on. Blocks are an expensive investment, but I can think of nothing more durable, versatile, economical (on a cost-per-use basis), pleasure-giving, and educational.

The Proper Roles

Adair Lara

When the babies were born—first a girl, then a boy—my husband Jim and I were confident that we could bestow on our children enlightened views of their sexual roles.

We began by being very careful to set the proper examples. Far from collapsing in front of the TV with a beer, Jim did all the shopping, cooking and sewing. "Anybody who can read can sew," he declared, and made the baby a pair of red crawlers, then moved on to making pillows. All our friends got pillows for Christmas.

It seemed to work. When Patrick was 3 and another boy ripped his pants, Patrick said sympathetically, "You should get your daddy to fix that for you."

I couldn't tinker with the carburetor or put a new deck on the house, being as inept in those areas as in the kitchen, but I could catch and throw and ride a bike pretty well. I was the one who taught Patrick to choke up on the bat and step into his swing, while Jim taught Morgan how to sew and make tuna casseroles.

We were so liberal that we were prepared in advance to accept any aberration. The kids could come to us and confess to be attracted to three-toed tree sloths, and we'd not only understand—we'd more than understand. We'd read all the right literature, find them a support group, join the Parents of Kids Who Want to Marry Three-Toed Tree Sloths. We'd serve cookies to the young sloths who came calling and revel in our broad-mindedness.

All of this, this gentle eddying stream of parental enlightenment, was a waste, a roar of sound on the tiny, deaf ears of the little stereotypes we were raising.

I have on a sheet of paper an early but typical dinner conversation across our enlightened table. Morgan, 4, remarked over her papaya, "Patrick looked like a girl all day today. That's a girl's sweater."

Patrick, 3, was incensed. "I looked like a *boy*," he said. "I have a boy's round face and a boy's round hand."

We gave Patrick a doll. He used it as a launching pad for his Hot Wheels.

Morgan took one look at the other girls in preschool and came home to ask, with an accusing stare, where her dresses were.

I would have taught her to step into her swing, too, but she wasn't interested. Now she's 12, and wears tons of makeup on her already perfect face. She goes to parties and aces the latest dances but shoots the basketball like a girl, or as she imagines a girl does it, which is badly. Her friend Marjanne takes her out for Saturday morning manicures and expensive haircuts.

Patrick, 11, speaks in a low voice and is always looking for something he can set fire to. "Do you need this Crisco, Mom?" He and his friend Gino sit in the backseat asking each other if they'd rather die from being stabbed or shot or eaten by a shark.

These days Morgan has taken to giving me advice on makeup, even dabbing peach eye-shadow on my lids as the car wheels around curves en route to a party. She is sure I can be taught how to be more of a girl if I would just concentrate and not fidget so much, and let her take me shopping.

Patrick, meanwhile, grabs his dad's apron away from him and drags him to the ball field, showing him how to use two hands to keep the ball from falling out of his mitt.

They figure it's an uphill battle, getting us to embrace our proper roles, but they'll keep at it.

"Being a father in this new age is a difficult task because we have no role models."

—John McCutcheon

Sally Rosloff and family.

A New Frontier

Sally Rosloff

Sometimes my husband and I feel that we are trying to go where no parents have gone before. Like the Star Trek ship Enterprise, we are venturing into a new frontier, that largely uncharted territory, "nonsexist parenting."

Our son is now eight, our daughter four and a half, and there was never any question that they would be raised nonsexist. Cooper and I met as volunteers for the Equal Rights Amendment campaign in the early '80s. Just friends then, I overheard him say, "So, boys and girls are raised with completely different expectations and then when they grow up they're supposed to find someone, marry, be intimate and share the same bed with someone who might as well be a Martian." How extraordinary, I thought, he understands sexism as clearly as I do.

Two years later we married and a little over a year after that we were pregnant. Suddenly we realized that it was one thing to philosophize, another to be facing a real baby. Just how were we supposed to go about it?

It boiled down to roles, those sets of predefined behavior that hang on people like ill-fitting clothes. We wanted none of it, no pink and blue, no tools and trucks versus dolls and tea sets, no coos and cuddles versus rough and tumble mock battles. We decided if we did nothing else, we would let our baby's personality be our guide. We would get to know this new person, what she or he liked/didn't like, how she or he chose to interact with the world, regardless of anatomy. We agreed not to expect anything of this child based on society's notions of what it means to be a boy or girl.

When we told people we were having a boy, they replied: "Now you can get ready ahead of time and decorate the nursery." "I never had brothers; I wouldn't know what to do with a boy." "I have three boys and it's Grand Central Station; I wish I had girls." "It's easier to raise boys, you don't have to worry about them as much." "I have a boy and I hope the next is a girl, I've always wanted a girl." Once when someone beamed with approval on hearing my firstborn was a boy, I walked away shaken, connecting in that moment to the women throughout history whose lives depended on bearing boys.

Like most new parents, we prepared for the baby ahead of time. The house we moved to when I was five months pregnant had race car wallpaper in one of the bedrooms; we scraped it off, painted the walls white, bought yellow and white bedding, and chose infant clothing in a rainbow of colors with patterns of balloons and teddy bears rather than trains and trucks.

Since I knew nothing about raising boys (having had no brothers) I had no preconceptions and was determined not to acquire any. I figured knowing nothing about boys was actually a plus; I planned to take my cues from him. But I had an inkling the room wouldn't always be neat and tidy.

Another thing we did ahead of time was choose a name. We wanted a unisex name, but none appealed. In the end, we chose the name of Cooper's father, who had died three months after we married. But that was just the first name; we also deliberated over the last name.

When we married, we each kept our names; neither of us liked the sound of them hyphenated. For children, we didn't like giving them hyphenated names because what happens when Jane Jones-Doe marries John Green-Brown? Finally, we decided on my last name. Cooper didn't feel particularly attached to his name; he had a small extended family while I had a large one that got together frequently for reunions and visits. I think, too, he liked the idea that our son would be carrying my family name.

A family member objected that a boy identifies with his father and if they don't have the same last name he might feel rejected. We didn't take this objection seriously.

Eventually the big day came and, wouldn't you know it, the minute he popped out he looked like a little football player, almost nine pounds, muscled, healthy and big. All I could think was, "Football over my dead body! If he is to be athletic let it be tennis, swimming, volleyball, martial arts, anything but football!" Now he's lean and lanky, the tallest in his class, and he has shown little interest in athletics; he has yet to learn to ride his bicycle without training wheels and prefers making up games with superhero action toys to playing catch. But of course, all I heard from everyone who saw him in the first few months was what a football player he was going to make.

As he grew from infancy to toddlerhood, we found it fascinating to follow our rule of interacting with him as a person, not as someone identified always as male. We told him he was good-looking rather than a big strong boy and we always comforted him when he cried. As he got older it became clear that he was a rambunctious, energetic kid. The stereotyping continued: "Boys are so active!" When confronted with an equally active girl, people either ignored it or labeled her a tomboy or became apologetic.

He did look very much the boy, always very tall for his age, and blue looked great on him with his Paul Newman eyes. But he also wore reds and purples and greens; we stayed away from sports team names on pajamas or camouflage clothing.

Our daughter was born when our son was three and a half. We could tell from the comments that almost everyone thought we wanted a girl; it was assumed that the perfect family was a boy first and a girl second. One woman told me how pleased I must be; when I asked her why, she said that an older brother can look out for his younger sister.

When the amniocentesis showed we would have a girl, one of my best friends revealed that she longed desperately for a girl. She gave a range of reasons, from wanting to buy a canopy bed to feeling that a daughter would be emotionally closer to her than her sons. I could never empathize.

I read an article by a woman with two boys who had completed her family but still yearned for a girl. She felt only a girl could evoke her own girlhood; she could pass on her Nancy Drew books, braid her daughter's hair and share secrets, slumber parties, and kitchen gossip.

The birth of my daughter summoned none of those feelings, most probably because of our conscious and deliberate effort to assume nothing about her. I remember a close family member who had raised only sons asking excitedly how it felt to have a daughter. It didn't "feel" anything. I didn't experience her differently than I had her brother. Except for when I changed her diaper, I didn't notice a difference. She was a new little person with whom I was falling in love, as I had her brother, and whom I was attempting to figure out.

This time I thought Cooper might want to give her his last name, but he didn't. We both preferred that our children have the same last name, so again, we passed on my family name, even though I warned Cooper that now he might get called "Mister My Last Name." It didn't faze him in the least.

We began very early to point out gender stereotyping and to spend time talking about it. Cooper and I shared child care routines according to our schedules and needs; he now does most of the school/bed/bath preparations.

Obviously, we could not put our son in dresses; but we also didn't want to put our daughter in them, or anything with bows, lace or ruffles. Our friends thought we were overreacting, but to us, little girls in dresses made them seem sweet, passive, and vulnerable. Besides, dresses are impractical for play. Just as I found I could not clothe myself in a traditional wedding dress for my wedding because of the images in my mind of ownership and femininity, I found I could not clothe my daughter in dresses.

Cooper and I agreed that when she asked for a dress we would comply. We knew she would reach that phase when young children notice how the world is divided and want to classify themselves accordingly. We are not happy that the most prominent division in our society is between the sexes. But she is learning how mom and dad feel about that too.

As it turned out, dressing her in unadorned playclothes, coupled with her tight curly hair, sturdy body and assertiveness, meant that she was often mistaken for a boy. We found that from birth, clothes are designed to send out the message blinking in neon "boy boy," "girl girl." There seems to be no in-between. It came as quite a surprise to us that complete strangers became annoyed when they mistakenly complimented my baby girl as a boy. One even chided me for having led her astray by not putting my daughter in the correct color!

Until just before her fourth birthday, our daughter seemed oblivious to gender typing. She knew because we talked about it that she was a girl and her brother a boy and why. But then she noticed strangers around her sometimes saying "Isn't he cute?" or "What curly hair he has!" Once she looked up indignantly and corrected them, saying, "I'm a SHE not a HE." Then came preschool where she made friends with girls who sometimes wore dresses, headbands, ponytails or nail polish. Suddenly aware that she did none of those things, she wanted to know why. She also asked if we could buy one of "those things that are open at the bottom" for her to wear.

And so it happened that just two weeks shy of her fourth birthday, we had our request for a dress and we honored it. Nothing too "froufrou," which so far is fine with our daughter. And I am learning to relax at the sight of her dressed as "a girl." At first she said, "Now people will know I am a girl. Girls wear dresses and boys don't." I told her I didn't think that fair, but she appeared unconcerned.

The first time I allowed the woman who cut our daughter's hair to put a bit of ribbon in it, our daughter was teasing her brother that she had a ribbon and he didn't. I told her that in our culture girls get to wear ribbons in their hair but boys don't. The next week, at a large family Passover dinner, she asked what the funny hat was that all the boys were wearing. I explained that it was a special hat for the service; she then asked why the girls weren't wearing them. I beamed at these powers of observation.

Our toys tend toward imaginative play; we have lots of blocks, legos, art supplies, puzzles, costumes, and the little people environments such as towns, zoos and airports. Most "girl" toys are not welcome in our house; they focus on hair, makeup, and fashion or are simply pretty objects to carry. What about dolls? As it turns out, our son hardly played with the one doll we bought for him, while our daughter seems interested in them. To us, that means that our son and daughter are both expressing their interests and following the cues in the world at large.

Our son discovered Ninja Turtles, Batman, Superman, X-Men and now Power Rangers through his friends. We allow him to watch the television shows about them but we do monitor it. He zeroed in on these male superheroes and molded his play around them. When still pregnant with our daughter, I worried what her models would be. Since her birth, a few have appeared on the scene: Ariel, the little mermaid; Belle from Beauty and the Beast; and Jasmine from Aladdin. While hardly equivalent to the male superhero hype, these characters offer some spunk and initiative and a starting place for us to talk.

At first I naively thought that our daughter could have the same models as our son, that she could watch them and be encouraged to take action as he had. But I learned that just as I had been discouraged when growing up by seeing only men in the world as news announcers, government officials, judges, bankers and businessmen, young children identify with the gender of the characters they are watching. Somewhere between three and four, my son's female playmates stopped being turtles to become Ariels or Snow Whites or princesses.

So far though, our daughter is not focusing her play on these characters. Unlike our son, she spends a lot of time at preschool on the play equipment, learning to cross the monkey bars, climb the jungle gym and swing and hang from the bars. She also loves to draw and leaf through books. Playing dress-up is a favorite but our son enjoyed that too. Her best friends are girls but occasionally they are joined by a boy; the play groups are more fluid at this point than they will be two or three years later.

I used to question my son as he progressed through nursery school to kindergarten about his playmates and games, worried that the boys and girls were separating. At parent/teacher conferences we always asked the teachers if the boys and girls played together, exploring ways that could be encouraged. It so happened there were few girls in his classes, making it hard to tell if a better balance would have made their play different.

Our son's best friend now is the girl across the street, who is two and a half years older. Her father is a full-time parent at home while her mother works full-time outside the home. Both her father and mother spend time with her; her toys range from a remote control dune buggy to lavender and pink legos. She chose to adopt the action model, buying action figures in addition to Barbie and Belle. She and our son play for hours on end making up and acting out stories with the latest superheroes. At school, she says she is teased and has a hard time making friends.

I'm not convinced that genes compel girls to play house and jump rope and boys to play cops and robbers. I still see most parents buying gender-typed toys based on the promotions in the media. Girls still get toys on nurturing (baby dolls, nursery and kitchen equipment), fashion (Barbie, dolls with hair to comb and clothes to accessorize) and beauty (makeup kits, bride costumes) while boys get action figures (Batman, Turtles, Superman), war toys (soldiers, weapons) and sports equipment. Occasionally, a boy likes playing with kitchen equipment, but the parents who do buy toys against type often observe that their kids revert, boys going back to trucks and girls to dolls.

There is not yet a critical mass for change. Kids are influenced by other kids and although roles have been changing in the past twenty years the basic message is still that boys act and girls react, boys initiate and girls nurture. It suddenly occurred to me when my son was about four that I was not talking about these stereotypes with him and could be; I started with television commercials.

"Girl" commercials have a pink and white glow, with beaming blonde-haired girls exclaiming over the latest doll with hair to comb or clothes to decorate. "Boy" commercials are dark and machine-filled with a booming male voice announcing the latest racing cars, monsters or action figures. I asked our son to tell me if he ever saw boys and girls in the same commercial. I explained to him that many people think some toys are for boys only or for girls only and that there are certain colors for girls and boys. I told him that all toys and colors are for both girls and boys. In the following months, I mentioned it occasionally, talking about what the different toys or games were and why they supposedly were only for boys or girls. Eventually, he too began to see what gender differences television was promoting.

Recently, a commentary appeared in our newspaper by a nine-year-old girl, castigating the people who write for television and those who manufacture toys for leaving girls on the sidelines. I called the family together to read it aloud and invite comment. I hoped to inspire empathy and perhaps even indignation in our son. Though he understands now that female characters are often there to be rescued or look sexy, he is not the one left out—but his sister is. He understood the message but thought girls were better represented than the writer of the commentary claimed. I decided I needed to talk about these things even more.

Communication has proved as important as treating each child as an individual. We now talk about stereotypes all the time, and not just sexist ones. The older our children get, the more fun we have asking them what they think. We take nothing for granted. One day, our daughter said to us that only the girls could look at the toys in her preschool cubby. Cooper and I exchanged looks. I asked her why. She replied that Benjamin had punched her. I asked if Joshua had punched her. She said he hadn't and that he could look at her toys. "Oh," I said to her, "you mean *people* who don't punch you can look at your toys." Yes, she meant people.

A lot of what we do crosses over into just plain parenting. We listen, talk, acknowledge feelings, set limits, pay attention, deal with needs and have lots of hugs and kisses, but we do all this regardless of who is the boy and who the girl.

Our son likes building forts and wants to be a scientist but we don't classify this as a boy activity. We know he also loves to read and write stories, is very bright, and cries when sad. Our daughter prefers shopping to hiking but she joins her brother in building the fort.

At a family gathering a cousin whom we hadn't seen for a while watched our daughter laughing and giggling with Cooper and asked if she was a Daddy's girl. I didn't know what to say; our daughter is just as likely to play with me and our son at the same age was just as likely to play with his father.

Early on we worried: Would our daughter be damaged since she didn't wear a dress until age four? Would our son not be tough enough for the harsh realities of the world out there? Would they feel too different from their playmates? But we are already seeing the results: teachers, friends and relatives all tell us that our children are bright, inquisitive, responsible and happy. We must be doing something right.

Eight years into parenting finds us more secure in our choices. Raising our kids without roles allows us to tune in to who they really are; a side benefit is learning more about who we are. We still wish there were others close by to share ideas and support. When I overhear statements like "You're not going to run around and get into trouble like your brother; no, you're a girl" (said to a two-month old), I'm angry. But then our son asks, "Is it against the law for men to wear dresses?" and I smile, ask him if he wants the short or the long answer, and continue creating our new frontier together.

"My parents did not have differing expectations for their girls and boys and always encouraged each of us to reach the limits of our capacities and put them to useful service. My brothers cleaned and made up beds as my sister and I did, and I learned how to wax cars and change tires as they did. I played with cars and trains far more than dolls and still can't sew worth a dime..."

—Marian Wright Edelman,
The Measure of Our Success

Robyn Parnell and son Eli Wagnell.

What's In a Name? Ask My Pal, Barry

Robyn Parnell

Girls should have strong names.

"Why?" my husband asks.

"For obvious reasons," I answer.

"Strong how?"

"The look; the sound. The meaning. Tenacious, bold names. Strong names."

We make a list of names we like. Sounding them in my mind, I look up their definitions in a "baby names dictionary." Sincerely though subjectively, I cross out names whose meanings I deem weak or frivolous.

My son could never be a Bart or a Kurt. There will be enough of those in his life. Being a son rather than a daughter will steer him toward Bartness without being burdened by such a name. Boys' names should have soft borders, gentle boundaries. The currently popular Matthew, Ryan, and Christopher are deceptive. Those names sound gentle around the edges, but, to me, they are Barts in trendy sheeps' clothing.

I scan the baby names book, which I received (along with an iron, an environmentally incorrect can of aerosol spray starch, and an apron) as a joke from a friend for my wedding. This book helps me in my work, which is writing short stories. I keep it in the reference section of my bookcase, along with thesauri and dictionaries. When I have difficulty naming a character, when a character's name must *mean* something, I reach for it.

This child deserves to have a name of its own. No numerals following the last name and no Junior. I have kept my birth name (those who use the term maiden name in our house are given a mop and a dustrag), the same way my husband has kept his. However, I've yet to hear someone ask him to explain the fact that his pre- and post-marital surname are the same. Its immutability is assumed.

Our child will have her or his own surname: two syllables, one from my husband's last name and one from mine.

"That's great! After all, if you're going to be a family, why be one or the other? Why not be something new, something unique, which, in fact, you are? If no one ever did anything different, there would be no traditions."

Friends and relatives (all female, now that I think of it, and all who, for various reasons and with varying amounts of enthusiasm, declined to make such changes themselves) have spoken in this way in support of our decision. A few suggest that 1) for the sake of simplicity, 2) with regard to (if not respect for) practicality, and 3) considering the limited storage capacities of both the human brain and computerized school registration forms, my husband and I should also assume the surname we will give our child.

So that we three will be the _____ family.

Three persons; one household; one last name? Catchy idea.

"We'll think about it," I say. This response seems to generate more positive feedback than, "We've considered it, but we each like our own." Or, "It would be a hassle to change. So what if they're different? Ultimately, what's in a name?"

Plenty, according to the baby names book, which follows a format similar to other books I've seen. The names are separated by gender, the girls' section usually (chivalrously?) preceding the boys'. Names are listed alphabetically, followed by the nation or language of origin, definitions, and nicknames or variations.

Calla (Greece) "Beauty." Cal, Callie, Cally.

More often than not, along with a personality trait or two, the definitions include a reference to appearance and form. Especially the girls' names.

Lian (Chinese) "Graceful willow."

I picture prospective parents flipping through these books, considering names for their girl-child.

Mirabel (Latin) "Extraordinary beauty."

Linda (Spanish) "Pretty."

Nani (Hawaiian) "Beautiful one from heaven."

Tiffany (Greek) "Like the appearance of God."

Who would do this to their daughter?

For nearly half of the girls' names, there is something like the following:

Carla (German) "A feminine form of Carl."

There is never such a definition for boys' names. "Masculine" names are not defined in terms of an Other. There is never:

Anthony (Latin) "A masculine form of Antoinette."

Never.

I put the baby names book on the floor underneath a dictionary and use the books for a footstool while I type.

I work on a story in which a certain character is killed, his death caused by a family member. He is loutish, unintelligent, bad-tempered. I close my eyes and picture him lurking behind my computer monitor. I know exactly what he looks like, what he smells like. Unlike the sympathetic characters in my story, no name springs to my mind, though I instinctively know who he is *not*. He is not Matthew, Ryan or Dylan, so I get the names book and search for inspiration. I come upon Barry, and am mesmerized by the sound as I repeat it, over and over. It resonates in my skull, like a growl.

Barry (Gaelic) "Warlike; spearlike. Pointed."

Perfect.

Life Exercises (excerpt)

Naomi Feigelson Chase

Looking out Ruthie's window when I wake her for school, I see a corner of the sky, the color of an oyster shell. Tomorrow will be spring. The temperature is up to fifty, but the radio says it may drop this afternoon and snow is on the way. I can't decide how many sweaters the children should wear, or whether to insist on coats and boots.

Over cereal, Ruthie wants to know who the Montagnards are. She and Sam watched a TV show at Martin's that said the Montagnard children are dying from American herbicides used in the war.

"What are herbicides anyway?" Sam asks. "Could I have those two bananas instead of cereal?"

Ruthie explains that herbicides are poison for trees and claims one banana is hers.

"Why did we want to kill trees?" Sam settles for one banana.

"The soldiers had to get the trees out of the way so they could see the Vietnamese to kill them."

"What if there's another war before I'm grown up?" Sam asks. "Do you think there will be, Mom?"

I decide they should wear boots.

"There probably will be some other war," Ruthie tells him.

"If there is, I'm going to medical school."

This is news to me. "I didn't know you wanted to be a doctor."

"I don't but I'm not going to be killed in some dumb war."

"I'll take you to Canada," I promise.

"I might be too old for you to take me."

"You could be a teacher. They didn't get drafted," Ruthie tells him. "All the guys at New Trent got out of the draft by being teachers. Do you think that's fair, Mom?"

"Do I think what's fair?"

"That some guys should get out and others should get drafted and get killed."

"No, it's not fair."

"So why were you a draft counselor?"

"I thought I should help as many people as possible."

Ruthie is skeptical. "Well, that's good," she says. "But what about the guys who don't know they can get out? Do you know rich men used to pay poor men to fight for them? Three hundred dollars in the Civil War. Mrs. Harris told us."

"Three hundred?" says Sam. "That doesn't sound like much."

"Mrs. Harris says it was worth more then. Thousands."

God bless Mrs. Harris. She saves me a lot of research.

"I can't pay anybody but I'm getting out," Sam says. "And don't tell me it's not fair."

"It's fair for you, but it's silly to go to medical school. It's a lot of work. Besides, I thought you didn't like the sight of blood."

"There's more blood in the army. It's safer to be a doctor. Don't you think so, Mom?"

"I don't think we have time to discuss this now. What about tonight at dinner?"

"I think that's a bad reason to be a doctor," Ruthie says in the elevator. "Then you'll hate going to work. Like Mom."

"It's easy for you to say. You'll never be drafted."

"Maybe they'll be drafting women by the time I'm grown up. A lot of liberated women think women should be in the army."

"That's nonsense," I say. "What's liberating about being in the army?"

"Don't ask me," Ruthie answers. "I'm not going in any army. I'm going to counsel everyone not to be drafted. What's that called?"

"It's called being a nutty radical."

"I was asking Mom," Ruthie says.

"It's called draft resistance. Why is it nutty to be radical?" I ask Sam.

"Because they go around blowing up buildings and killing policemen and doing things like kidnapping Patty Hearst."

"Not necessarily. There are all kinds of radicals." How can I analyze this subject for Sam, or even for myself this early in the morning?

"Well, at least you're not one," he says to me. "Or are you?"

"Of course we are," Ruthie answers. "Women have to be radical."

I have just finished coating the chicken with egg and am shaking the first piece in a bag of flour when Ruthie comes in wearing her best torn jeans and favorite faded Indian shirt. She wants to help. I hand her the bag of flour. I love her outfit. I love her. I wish she would stay this age forever.

"Mom," she says, dropping a chicken leg in the bag and shaking it, "Sam woke me up last night to tell me the stabber was in his room."

"What did you do?"

"I told him the stabber wasn't a real person so he couldn't follow him." She takes another leg.

"And?" I ask.

"Sam said the stabber was in his room, real or not."

Oh, God or someone, please help me deal with this. Why does everyone think they're being followed?

Sam is in the living room turning on the TV. Ruthie has finished flouring and I've started frying. "Mom," Sam hollers, "Nixon still has those tapes and he lied on his taxes."

"Sam," I holler back, "set the table."

"I gotta see this first."

"See it second. First the table."

"He's gonna get impeached." Sam comes into the kitchen for the knives and forks. "Don't you think so?"

"Not for lying on his taxes," Ruthie says. "Everybody does that."

"Everybody does not cheat on their taxes," I say sternly.

"Dad says it's just stretching the truth."

Sam disagrees. "I think it's really lying," he says, as he sets the table and goes back to the news.

I need to get this straight. "Does your father say that about Nixon, or about everybody?"

"Dad says everybody cheats a little on their taxes."

"I don't think that's true."

"I hate it when you and Dad fight," Ruthie says.

"We're not fighting. I don't think what he told you is correct."

"It just makes me uncomfortable." Ruthie shrugs her shoulders.

"I'm sorry if it makes you feel bad, but even divorced people have a right to disagree. I don't cheat on my taxes. It's just too cynical to say that everybody bends the truth. I'm sure that's not really what your father means."

"Maybe it's just New Yorkers," Ruthie says, trying to find a way out.

"Nixon isn't from New York," Sam says, walking into the dining room and sitting down at the table. "I think I'm going to be a vegetarian like Ruthie. How come you're eating chicken?"

"You can't be a purist about everything," she says. "Besides I need the protein for my brain."

"I'm going to be a purist but I'm not going to be a radical."

"Why not?" I ask.

"I want to be like Dad," he says. "I want to be normal. Could I give my chicken to Captain and President?"

"Dad wouldn't do that," Ruthie says.

"Not all grown-ups are crazy. Some people really just lead normal lives," I say.

"Who?"

"We do."

"Then why are we divorced?" Sam asks.

"Normal people get divorced."

"No they don't."

"I know you're upset about the divorce, but we should talk about it."

"I'm not upset. And I don't want to talk about it." Sam gets up and leaves the room.

"It's so hard to have a conversation around here," Ruthie says.

I tell her Sam is trying to figure out how to be a man. "It's hard. They're not supposed to feel. And if they do, they're not supposed to show it. We have to help him."

"Men!" she says. "Women are oppressed and all that, but really, I think we have it easier." She knocks on Sam's door. "Hey, MVP," she says, "why don't we take some chicken outside so Captain and President can have it for dinner?"

Sam opens his door a crack. "I guess they can't afford to be vegetarians," he says.

"Sam could be a radical yet," Ruthie reassures me.

Mace for the Child Molester

Li Min Hua

"What a big chemistry set Santa brought!"
    I exclaimed to Michael, 10,
son of the chemist turned dean,
    when we went nextdoor
for spicy Christmas cake.

Michael beamed as his dad peered
    proudly over half-rims.

Mary, 6, nudged to show me her gift.
    "And what a cute nurse's kit,"
I added with a patron's smile.

"Doctor's kit," the housewife intruded;
    "tell him it's a doctor's kit, Mary,"
Mary's mother repeated even as she fetched us
    pieces of her best minced meat pie.

Guys and Dolls

Jean Tepperman

"I did buy my little boy a doll," protested a mother at the cooperative preschool parents' meeting, "but he won't play with it." The workshop leader answered by telling a story.

"Recently," she said, "I visited a friend who had a little boy. I brought along a doll, but not just a plain doll. It was in a basket, with changes of clothes and some other equipment.

"My friend's son played with it the whole time—the mother was amazed. It worked because there were enough other things with the doll to make the experience interesting."

The workshop was on gender-fair education, developed in response to the 1992 American Association of University Women's blistering study, "How Schools Shortchange Girls."

The parents, a racially mixed group of mothers and fathers, sat perched on child-size chairs and listened intently. How important do they think it is, I wondered, to find ways to get boys to play with dolls? Then from behind me came a discreet side-conversation: "Well, I think it would be good for boys to play with dolls," a mother whispered. "It would help them learn to be more nurturing." "Well, I am, and I never did play with dolls," a father replied, defending himself.

In the preschool years, the workshop leaders said, children learn through play. By playing with dolls, building with blocks, or measuring cookie ingredients, kids learn skills and gain the confidence that comes from experience. By trying out activities and roles, little kids start to define themselves.

But a preschool is as full of gender stereotypes as a 1950s sitcom. Girls are playing with dolls in the housekeeping corner and the dress-up area. Boys are building with blocks and zooming trucks around.

"I believed sex differences were all social conditioning until I had kids," I've heard countless parents say. When kids as young as 3 seem to gravitate so strongly to sex-stereotyped activity and behavior, can you fight it?

Instead of trying to fight it, this workshop was talking about expanding all kids' experiences, skills, and senses of possibility—and about strategies that work.

In a cooperative preschool, for example, when an "undersea world" activity that involved stuffed animals and fantasy play was brought to the area where the boys played with blocks, the girls came along and participated. While girls and boys were building undersea caves, they were absorbing pre-math skills and competence in mechanics. That kind of play may help them later to withstand the free fall in self-confidence, the "learned helplessness," that the AAUW study documented in teenage girls.

Even the most well-meaning parents and teachers unconsciously reinforce sexism. The AAUW found that most teachers—even in preschools—pay more attention to boys than to girls. Boys get more chances to speak, more praise and suggestions, more hugs.

Why? Parents and teachers in this workshop thought they knew: Boys were more demanding—and the girls already seemed to be doing better than the boys without so much attention.

The AAUW study points out that the preschool curriculum tends to emphasize things girls were already good at—fine motor skills, language, cooperating in groups. "Boy" activities, like building with blocks, are optional activities girls might not choose unless they're encouraged to. The result, says the AAUW, is the girls "do not receive a full and balanced set of educational experiences."

The best part of the workshop was at the end when they gave examples of changes that expanded kids' experiences: Play-Doh in the toy kitchen, stuffed animals with the blocks, picture books about the adventures of girls—toys and books that give kids a fuller, richer sense of the possibilities for both sexes.

The workshop was exciting because it's part of a new push to tackle the powerful forces that shape sexism. These efforts show that we're not doomed to stunt the growth of future generations of kids. Parents and teachers can make practical changes that help kids learn a wider range of abilities—and the confidence that goes with them.

Imagine all those preschool boys giving dolls rides in their trucks, those teenage girls signing up for calculus. It's enough to make you wonder if the rest of us grownups might have more potential than we have hitherto shown.

"Every individual's life is diminished when human characteristics are arbitrarily assigned to one sex or the other."

—from *Equal Their Chances*

Ellen Farmer with Janna and Scott.

The Difference Between Boys and Girls

Ellen Farmer

"Children need interesting mothers"

—Marge Frantz

A self-confident six-year-old races across the playground on a cool spring day. She is delighted to be outdoors moving freely, deciding how to make the most of her recess. She runs up to the girls from her class she counts as friends. The tallest, oldest one turns to her, unhappy at the interruption. "Go away—we're busy," she says with her eyes. The younger child does not take the hint, but instead suggests a game of freeze tag.

"I'm reading *this list*," says the older girl. "These girls are coming to my overnight." She continues to read the list, and the younger girl's name is not on it. The group marches away from her—smug, insular, secure in their togetherness. They are seven years old.

I get this story from my daughter a few weeks later while I'm driving the car. Clearly, my daughter has been put in her place. She tells the story in an unusually quiet voice—a voice timid with shame and humiliation. It sounds to me as if she is resigned to this kind of treatment, feeling she has no allies in the adults or girls at her school. I'm so angry I want to seek immediate revenge, but I feel paralyzed—I'm supposed to be grown up. How is a feminist to behave in the face of this raw "female" power?

A few months before this incident I attempted to get my daughter's first-grade teacher interested in playground dynamics, but she disarmed me in her pleasant manner by saying, "I never see that kind of behavior in the classroom." Recess was clearly not her responsibility. Apparently, this girls' version of *Lord of the Flies* would be officially ignored.

An ultra-feminist friend of mine tells me of a girl who visits frequently and seems to delight in sharing titillating stories about girls at her school. She gets a thrill out of describing one who's really fat and one with a really big nose. My friend hears a familiar tone in her voice that greatly disturbs her, but she doesn't know how to respond. She wants to get to know this nine-year-old neighbor, and it won't help if she comes across like a fuddy-duddy.

What enormous changes of heart have we gone through in the period between our own girlhood and our current woman-loving feminism? How did the message to compete with other girls and disregard their feelings get imbedded so strongly in us as young children? And what steps did we take to exorcise it? I remember being told by "girls-in-the-know" that I was cute and smart but not daring enough to be in the top group. They told me I would hold the others back because I was afraid of getting in trouble. I became extremely shy and self-conscious at school and played with younger kids in the neighborhood. When I got to my 30s I remember I felt permitted to love, trust, and appreciate women. It was a revelation to me that a fat woman or one with a big nose might have some value in my life.

Why didn't anyone say anything to me as a child? Did the grown-up women around me support me, but the influence of my 7-8-9-year-old peers was stronger?

As a feminist with a daughter, I'm searching for a strong, exciting message to give young girls to combat the adult/media messages they seem to absorb *in utero* about how to treat each other. I feel their cruelty toward one another is something we hope is a stage, but it's time to ask why. Why are we allowing our daughters to perpetuate this painful pecking order? What role does the elementary school have in shaping a safe climate for children's social interactions, and how much is up to the parents to interfere?

I believe this problem is related to the lip service we pay to embracing diversity. We learned social survival skills on the playground. In particular, what we learned was to aim for the top clique. If we couldn't make it "in," we still had to acknowledge the power these girls wielded. Embracing diversity implies a level playing field where all children share center stage from time to time. It implies mutual respect and mutual appreciation of a variety of cultural experiences.

It's true that embracing diversity and learning to enjoy our differences can't hold a candle to the excitement of being most popular. Kids are still being left out—from the ones who don't know the ropes and will never learn them, to those whose feminist parents deliberately stymie their efforts to participate in classic girl power games. I'm saddened that this issue isn't an obvious concern to the teachers and parents at the "progressive" public school my children attend. I have talked to individual teachers who are aware of the problem, but it would take a critical percentage of teachers, aides, playground supervisors, office staff, and the principal to change school standards.

My dilemma is—do I myself teach my daughter about the world of cliques so she'll recognize what's going on or do I leave her alone to fend for herself and hope she's one of those kids who quickly finds the clique silly? I do believe that feminism has made strides in supporting sports teams for girls so they have alternative arenas for competition. But we must address first of all our tired definition of "girls" and stop taking it for granted that females treat each other this way. We can't help children embrace diversity until we help them find ways to sincerely care about each other, one by one, girl to girl.

Because of feminism, I have come to realize that all forms of oppression are connected and must be challenged. I became a feminist in 1971 at the age of 19. Many issues have had personal significance—birth control, choosing to have children, equal access to education, equal opportunities at work, accessible child care, unlearning sexism and homophobia.

Because of my feminist values, I truly believed a man could do anything a woman could do as a parent. So I pumped extra breast milk from day one and gave my children's dad the bottles so he could hold the baby to his bare chest and bond. (It worked.) And I assumed he could cook meals, drive the children to day care, change diapers, read to the kids, etc., etc. I felt absolutely certain this egalitarian household would be an ethically sound place for my children's upbringing, but the stresses took an emotional toll. I think both my husband and I needed someone to talk to, someone who wasn't obsessing over yet another case of pink eye. Therefore, we sought out other adults. Eventually we developed a two-household family structure for the children.

When I recovered my equilibrium, I realized this home style was the perfect feminist solution to the constraints and assumptions of the nuclear family. The children see their father half the week as nurturer and caregiver. They see both of us with careers. And I have a great deal of time to pursue interests, such as writing and music, that I might have had to give up as a full-time mom. When I describe our compatible solution to parents and teachers, they seem impressed and willing to accept the notion, but the ghosts-of-divorces-past linger in some people's memories. There is a stereotype about children from "broken" homes— that they all must be insecure and upset. Even though we've devised a family structure that really works for all of us, the doubts and assumptions of others may dog us forever.

Over the past five years, as our son grew to be ten and our daughter six, I've learned to expect very different patterns from parents of sons and parents of daughters. Parents of sons seem to have more of a devil-may-care attitude, not always requesting good manners and tidiness, while parents of girls are more wary about where and how their children play. We have not raised a sweet, docile, future sorority sister with perfect manners and a charming attitude. As an infant she was surrounded and nurtured by my lesbian housemates. She was delighted by the energy of 4-year-old boys constantly running through her room (compared to the relative calm her brother experienced as an infant). She soon developed a contagious laugh and a vivid, playful imagination. All her loud, boisterous, active ways were grandly applauded by the dykes around her. And no one—absolutely no one—trained her to be a young lady. Will she survive? What follows is a comparison of the world of boys and the world of girls as I have observed them.

The Boys

My son is a feminist's dream. He has a conscience, a kind nature, and a willingness to consider the feelings of others. He had the benefits of being an only child for four years in an idealistic household.

After watching my son and his friends play together from the time they were two years old, I realized their curiosity would push them to destroy almost anything in the name of "science." Some of the "conscious" parents I knew encouraged this behavior because the books said not to squash kids' egos. But sometimes the boys got too loud, sometimes too aggressive, sometimes too taken with smashing perfectly good toys into smithereens for the sheer power of the act.

What stymied me was other parents' ability to tune all this out. Why weren't they reacting, setting limits, reaching a level where the kids' behavior was intolerable? Did they just pretend not to notice when other parents were around? For me, learning to parent my first child was like clawing my way through the jungle with blinders on. I perceived few clearings and very few moments of enlightenment. I did get one click of intuition, however, and it went like this:

We can have house rules! (ah ha!)
They can be simple.
At our house we don't call names.
At our house we don't destroy things.
At our house you need to get the other kids' permission if you're going to play shooting, chasing, tickling games.

And it's okay for me to ask you to quiet down.
And you can't hit me.
And that's that.

I watched with some alarm as some of the boys I knew hit their moms. I thought: how do you stop wife-beating if you let them abuse you as a mother? I didn't have any idea how to say this out loud to these otherwise mature, adult women. I began to see that the moms were treating their two-year-old boys like future men. These women were already resigned to their sons' power. They deferred to their little masters. When the boys were with me, I gave myself permission to stop any woman-hating behavior and talk to them about the need to respect women. I never got a shred of advice on this topic from Dr. Spock, parenting classes, or my friends.

The Girls

I'm not sure why girls seem so interested in hurting each other's feelings. Are they imitating their mothers, their teachers? Do they hear this on T.V.? Where are the roots of this evil?

When I finally figured out I could invent house rules for the boys, the rules seemed so logical. I never could figure out what to say to the girls. Jude-the-thoughtful-feminist says, "There is a world of difference between saying *Be nice* and *Don't be mean*," the latter a far more consistent message from a feminist mom. But kids have a hard time remembering negative messages, which always follow some (probably thrilling) misbehavior.

What worries me is that primary school-age girls already exhibit the woman-hating inherent in this society, and we ignore them. We know that one of the tools of survival is learning to compete with other girls for perceived goodies.

Contrary to sugar-and-spice mythology, girls *are* competitive. Because we don't encourage them enough in appropriate areas of competition and loud, boisterous play or sports, they get their power fix by one-upping other kids in social situations, especially other girls. All of this is painful to watch because the ones who "behave" and act like "young ladies" are probably the sneakiest of all—destined for this weird definition we have of female success. Some are genuinely kind and loving, but they have to learn to play the game to get by. The ones who've been trained to be forthright, whom we support in their assertiveness, are brutally teased for being unsophisticated by the "girl police."

My hope is that thanks to feminism, many more doors are open to our daughters and their friends. They don't need to compete over the favors of men in order to survive, as women did earlier in this century.

Hopefully, we'll devise ways to help them develop team approaches to life's challenges. Showing our daughters how to stop oppression by building coalitions and working for justice doesn't have to be dull. If we act from our hearts, they may get excited about respecting all kinds of people—even other girls—and creating a stronger, more peaceful society.

Teachers have to encourage creative, assertive behavior when girls speak out. It starts in the home, where Daddy (or other male figures) must *mentor* rather than *baby* their daughters, and mothers must not be so humble about the complexities of family management. (I am assuming that mothers are still doing most of the family management in this society.) Just as we groom our boys for teamwork and leadership, we must help our girls develop their inner strength as they rise to positions of power and influence. If we continue to let them focus their tremendous energy on hurting one another while we look the other way, we lose a great opportunity for character-building and let ourselves off the hook as role models. Everyone loses.

Soaring

Marilyn Krysl

"I've enrolled the kids in Intro to Soaring," my friend Carol says. We're having some white wine in my backyard, catching up. Carol and I came of age in the Sixties, but she had her kids late. Now Sky and Ocean are thirteen and eleven. You want me to tell you which is the girl and which is the boy? These are unisex kids, their mother is an equal opportunity employer.

"Soaring?" I say. Last year it was Zen Basketball. Before that Vision Quest. For Carol, activism and self-improvement go hand in hand. While she organized the local grape and lettuce boycott and a letter campaign against Red Dye No. 2, she was doing TM. She rallied against ROTC in the morning, ran the counseling center for draft resisters in the afternoon, and studied Chinese at night. Though she's a blonde who sunburns in the shade, she was once president of CORE. This in a community of 80,000 where there was one black family, a professor of Afro-American Studies on a one-year contract and his wife. Carol got two hundred and fifty people to parade down to City Hall and demand the city integrate its personnel. She was once, simultaneously, chair of the local Americans for Democratic Action, the ACLU, the Democratic Women's Caucus, and the PTA, and at the same time she took Assertiveness Training, Botany and Auto Mechanics.

Me, I'm all for changing the system, but I didn't think I needed to practice Tai Chi. I don't want to bare my breasts or my soul in Encounter Group. I like myself the way I am. I think I'm fine, it's The Powers That Be who need bodywork. It was Tricky Dick who needed Maracapy Dance Movement Therapy. It's Jeanne Kirkpatrick and Phyllis Schlafly, it's not me.

Carol thinks otherwise. She pickets for the disabled and for abortion rights at the same time she gets Rolfed and does Primal Scream Therapy. She organizes free Financial Planning classes for single mothers, then goes off into the woods for Outward Bound Endurance Testing. Her kids have chalked up credits in Cardiopulmonary Resuscitation, Indonesian Cookery, Beginning, Intermediate and Advanced Senegalese, Western Wildflowers and Sign Language.

Now Intro to Soaring.

"Isn't trying to fly dangerous?" I say. "Shouldn't they be in the library instead?"

Carol shakes her head. "They need life skills," she says.

Life skills? These kids have them already. Their mother sat in the grass between Jerry Rubin and Timothy Leary. Sky and Ocean lay down with their mother in front of buses. Ocean's first complete sentence was "We shall overcome." These kids can sit in a circle holding hands indefinitely and not get bored. If their mother called an ice cream boycott to protest exploitation of dairy workers, Sky and Ocean would give up Chocolate Fudge Nut Ripple without a whimper. They keep a bag of gorp and plastic bottles of drinking water at hand, and they dress for arrest. At any moment their mom may decide to pile them into somebody's Volkswagen camper and head for the Capitol.

"They've got life skills," I say, "but can they read? Do they know about prime numbers?"

"Don't worry," Carol says, "they were both reading at three."

"I know they're smart cookies," I say. "I was wondering about their preparation."

"For college?"

I nod.

"They can take College Prep," Carol says. Then she changes the subject. "Did you know they've both got black belts in karate now?"

Karate. Sky and Ocean have been through Nonviolence Training six different times. Gentleness and due process have been impressed upon them. When Sky got the whole seventh grade class at the Junior High to petition the principal until she met their demand for a vegetarian lunchroom, this kid personally wrote the principal a thank you note. Now Karate?

"Aren't they going to be confused?" I say. "What if Sky forgets and whaps a cop next time you block the entrance to Rocky Flats? Isn't this a contradiction?"

"The human animal is a very complex organism," Carol says. "They can handle contradiction. Besides, I'm working on a plan to convert Rocky Flats from plutonium triggers to lingerie."

This woman's got optimism like it was estrogen. Startling improvements are just around the corner. The country's 586 toxic waste sites will be cleaned up within the year, she's working on this. The heads of multinationals will discover their error and turn their assets over to the Third World. She's working on that too. Meanwhile she goes door to door for Safehouse, gets asbestos out of the schools, and studies Zulu.

Me, I'm working on reading a sleazy novel. I think people can improve too much. Do I really need Right Brain Left Brain Complementarity courses? Will I fall behind if I can't do Baby Massage?

"But will they be able to pass the SATs?" I say. "Can they write the biographical essay?"

"Don't worry," Carol says. "They need expanding now." She's been reading Huxley's *Doors of Perception* again, I can tell. "Stimulation's good for them," she says.

"What about burnout?" I say.

"Not likely," Carol says. "But if they do, they can take Integrative Rebirthing with me. I'm thinking of enrolling us all in Politics of South Africa after Christmas," she adds. There's a glazed-over look in her eyes, she's got plans. "And Understanding Foreign Policy."

"Your kids need Physics and Spelling," I say. "It's the Senator who needs Understanding Foreign Policy."

Carol looks at me. She smiles. "Someday they'll be the Senator," she says.

Joan Dickenson and family, 1974.

What Goes without Saving

Joan Dickenson

My father was the only man in a houseful of women, but he always left the toilet seat up after he peed. No one ever reproached him. His rights outweighed ours. Meals were timed for his convenience. Rooms were cleaned on a schedule that ensured he never had to enter a messy one. His food was bought, prepared, and served. His clothes were collected from the hamper, washed, ironed, mended, and returned to the drawer, exquisitely folded.

This picture sounds like the portrait of a despot, but my father was a mild and gentle man. Was he the architect who placed himself at the center of our household, or was the arrangement my mother's doing? Probably the two conspired to produce the fatherly god whose worship was unquestioned. In my family's theology, "breakfast with Daddy" was a sacrament.

I was the youngest of three girls. Carol was born in 1934 and Susan in 1938. As my mother tried to produce the longed-for son over the next ten years, she had four miscarriages. When I was finally born, in 1948, she was forty.

My father always maintained that he didn't care about gender; it was my mother who longed for a son. She maintained that she wanted a son not for herself but for him, "to carry on the family name"—his name. Inwardly, I believe, she wanted a son to prove herself a legitimate, successful woman. My existence was the mark of her failure.

Overtly, my parents taught me I could do anything. If I practiced, I could be a concert pianist. If I studied, I could earn a Ph.D. from Harvard, *summa cum laude*. If I continued writing, someday I'd be a famous author. In literature, being a girl was no handicap.

But my father's reading habits belied his encouragement. Although he read three or four mysteries a week, he hardly ever read mysteries by women—British women never and American women rarely. Nor would he read lady novelists. "Why do so many lady novelists have three names?" he would ask. "Mary Roberts Rinehart, Dorothy Canfield Fisher..."

I accepted his dislike of women writers as a taste, no more remarkable than his aversion to olives. It had nothing to do with my writing career. I would not write British mysteries, I would never be a lady novelist, I would not use three names. I never connected myself with the writers my father refused to read. I didn't relate his literary preferences to the fact that when my mother returned to school and work, she had to hire someone to care for the house and me. My father's freedom and duty to his work were taken for granted. Also taken for granted was the primary job of every woman. I might become a mathematician or a world-class writer, but first, I'd be a wife and mother. The message was always "When you have your own husband and children," and in fact, my sisters and I obediently married young and quickly had kids.

Throughout my childhood, boys were exotic creatures who rarely appeared in our house. The absence of young males made men alien beings to my sisters and me. I never experienced any casual give-and-take with boys my age. I envied girls with older brothers, because they knew how to talk to boys. I never did. On the rare occasions when they spoke to me, I didn't know how to answer. A pleasant remark from a male classmate was enough to make me fall in love, simply on the basis that a boy had actually noticed me. So when I married, the only way I knew to act with a husband was the way my mother acted: defer to him, serve him, build the household around his needs, his schedule, the myth of his infallibility.

Then in 1980, I discovered feminism from Letty Cottin Pogrebin's book *Growing Up Free: Raising Your Child in the '80s*. I tried immediately to change the way I dealt with my children, but unfortunately, at age ten, nine, and eight, they were already past the most impressionable age.

Their pre-Pogrebin upbringing did contain some feminist fragments. At age four, for instance, the children graduated to the privilege of washing dishes, a task they continued to do into their high school years. But although the kids and I did the dishes, my husband rarely took a turn in the rotation. And the children didn't wash dishes out of feminist commitment; they washed them because I forced them to. They did housework only as an extension of my arm. When I eased the pressure, they quit.

I read Pogrebin with a basic misunderstanding. I thought that once we pointed out feminist truths to men, they'd say, "Oh, no, have I really been acting like a slaveholder? Let's sit down and figure out how to become equals in our marriage. Let me bring you a cup of coffee." But they didn't react with eagerness to change. In fact, they barely reacted at all. "Oh, really?" they said. "Women are actually human beings? How

54

interesting." No one gives up power without a struggle. Unfortunately, by the time I gathered enough power to mount a struggle, my children's basic assumptions were tattooed into their brains.

More important, I couldn't change my own behavior overnight. One of my mother's favorite sayings was "Do as I say, not as I do," uttered with a wry acknowledgment of her own shortcomings as a model. Like her, I discovered that children don't learn from formal instruction but from the unspoken assumptions that underlie their parents' acts. I may say repeatedly that women shouldn't be handmaidens to men, but then I hand my husband a sandwich on a plate. "Do you want hot sauce?" I ask.

The act of service feeds not only his physical hunger and emotional expectations but also some need in me. Evidently I need a man to validate my competence in homemaking—and more deeply, my womanhood. I don't like to admit this need; it makes me feel ashamed that I'm not strong enough. Sometimes I try to justify the service on the basis that my husband doesn't know how to nourish himself, forgets to eat, and often becomes sick and irritable from lack of food. Although there's some truth to this rationale, it diminishes us both and provides a disgraceful model for the children. Nor is it entirely accurate. If I'm not available, he doesn't starve. When I spent two months at a writers' retreat last spring, he thrived.

But the pattern we two have woven is the pattern that seems natural to our children. A woman standing at the stove stirring a pot will seem right to them, whether she's a lawyer, a civil engineer, a restaurant cook, or a paid houseworker worrying about the soup she'll stir for her own family later on.

I don't say our household is entirely traditional. Giving medicine, worming dogs, and caring for sick children are my husband's responsibility. So are cleaning toilets, defrosting refrigerators, vacuuming, and ironing. But an unorthodox division of labor doesn't make a feminist household. The vital question is not who does the cooking but who does the emotional work? Whose moods temper the air, who feels responsible for other people's state of mind, who takes the initiative in peacemaking, who intercedes in quarrels, who feels free to disappear from household activities when depressed, who keeps the meals coming regardless of mental state, who learns to put her temper on hold for a more convenient season, and does that season ever come?

My husband's moods color the atmosphere. A first-class evil mood turns the air black, like a heap of tires burning in the kitchen. Thick smoke fills the house. Every breath hurts. A common everyday bad mood turns the air merely gray, as if someone is burning leaves in the yard. A good mood, on the other hand, produces ordinary air, pleasant, breathable, and unremarkable. One doesn't notice being able to breathe; only the absence or fouling of the air draws attention.

My moods, no matter how intense they feel internally, don't have much effect on the air. At most, a little lavender puff tints the kitchen a minute, then dissipates. Nobody's breathing is impaired. No one even has to clear a throat.

Whereas women are trained to keep things pleasant, fatherly anger is an American tradition. How many times, in how many millions of families, have mothers and children conspired to avoid it? "You better fix that before Dad finds out" is a mantra for survival in the nuclear family. My husband can't understand why the children and I will go to enormous lengths to pull the car out of the ditch, or fix a broken windshield-washer, before he can find out about the disaster. His anger doesn't terrify *him*. Of course, when he does learn of these misdemeanors, he doubles the anger, furious that no one told him before. As a consequence, not of their conscious upbringing but of the unspoken assumptions of this house, my children follow parallel patterns. The boys are moody, unpredictable, and often openly angry; the girl keeps things pleasant. There are individual variations—one son is more equable than the other, and my daughter shows more anger than I do—but the patterns are there.

Apart from the rituals of anger, many of our household patterns are egalitarian. The children were raised in an atmosphere of respect for my work, both the unpaid writing I do at home and my job as a newspaper reporter. Unlike my parents' table, where my father sat at the head regardless of company or occasion, our table has no head. We eat buffet style—if not a feminist pattern, at least not a baronial one. Yet although the details are different—my father, for instance, never blew up but met misfortune with philosophy and humor—Dad remains the center around which other people revolve. In some form, that pattern will likely persist in my children's own homes.

My daughter is more of a feminist than my sons. No credit is due to me; raising female feminists isn't difficult. Our society rewards assertive women. On the other hand, it scorns sensitive men. With grief, I watched the local school teach my sons to hide their sensitive natures behind a conventionally masculine mask. Later, even more sadly, I watched the mask grow into their skin. Few men have the courage to give up the status conferred on them by an accident of birth.

I've done better feminist child-rearing in matters that are superficial, though still important. When I hear female screaming coming from the TV, I sing out, "Violence against women!" and now the kids notice it themselves. When we discuss news, music, art, movies, and local affairs, I consider every scrap of discourse in the light of its relation to women. The children have absorbed a feminist attitude toward public affairs and take delight in pointing out my occasional lapses into sexism. Understanding the unfunniness of anti-woman humor, they don't tell hurtful jokes. More than I did at their age, they take women's humanity for granted. I take comfort in their instincts. People's central beliefs lie not in what they say, but in what they take for granted, what goes without saying.

Besides, my sons don't leave the toilet seat up after they pee.

My Grandmothers, My Mother, My Children

Lucy Kemnitzer

I'm not a pioneer. I used to say I was culturally conservative, by which I meant that I live by the traditions I received as a child from my parents. But the term may be misleading. It's a point of pride for me to be the granddaughter of feminists. I never really knew them. My father's mother died when he was a teenager, and my mother's mother died when I was five. I have pieced together some things about the lives my parents led as children, and the lives my brother and I led, and the lives my children are leading, and the ways that my grandparents, my parents, and my brother and I approach the task of raising children.

Both of my grandmothers were professional women who came of age in the twenties. My mother's mother was a doctor who specialized in psychiatry, and my father's mother was a bacteriologist, a public health scientist.

My parents' childhoods were bizarre. My father hardly saw either of his parents; he and my aunt were cared for by a series of baby-sitters and cooks while my grandfather prospected for oil and carried on his business, and my grandmother attended meetings and political functions (she was also in Women's International League for Peace and Freedom, and The League of Women Voters) all around the state.

It was not merely that she was a busy professional woman: she had no time for her children at all. When she died young, my father had to care for himself, and his little sister was sent away to boarding school.

My mother's babysitters were clinically insane. She lived on the grounds of a mental hospital; she told me stories of people who received instructions from God through the radio and who had an occasional violent lapse. However, she told me just before she died that the worst experiences she had at the hospital were at the hands of a couple of psychiatrists.

I don't wish to be saying here that these intense occupations and dedication to public service are incompatible with raising children. I wish to say that my grandmothers found it hard to focus enough energy on their children. But they articulated their philosophies and lived their visions, and my parents' lives were enriched by their activities and the intellectual pitch their mothers set.

My father and my mother used the word "feminist" freely. They were Marxist feminists. They applied that reasoning to the problems I faced growing up. When I went to a Black school and complained that the students were not very friendly, my parents put it in perspective with the racism the other students experienced every day. The advice my parents gave me frequently amounted to taking on all the responsibility for changing society and demanding none of the perks.

However, my mother pushed me, exhorting me to take the hardest courses in school, to aim high. Both of them advised me not to take typing courses because it would limit me to secretarial jobs. (Bad advice. Not being able to type accurately meant I ended up working in factories at half the wage.)

I asked my father once why it was almost always men who were known as writers and artists, though among the children I knew it was mainly girls who liked to write and to draw. He told me it was because men controlled the economic system, men who decided who could and could not be published.

When I first came across the argument about whether mothers should work, it puzzled me. Mothers worked, in my experience, as much as fathers. I did time on the unemployment line with my mother, but it was my father who was more often not working, either because he was at the bottom of the list for railroad jobs, or later, because he was going to school. And fathers, in my experience, did childcare, cleaned, and cooked.

My mother's world was circumscribed by fear; my father's was not. My mother was fenced in by her sex; my father could and did and does go anywhere, among any people of any background, and speak freely as an equal. My mother always had to consider her vulnerability and contend with the notion that somebody might see her as fair game if she attempted to move freely and alone.

It hurt her deeply. And it meant that, though she strived to give me an optimistic and ambitious view of life, what she communicated was this fear, this sense of disempowerment and vulnerability. And in contrast to the ideology she voiced, I got from her a sense that women's lives ultimately were limited and inevitably dependent on the whims of men.

In some ways, I would be happy if I could do for my children what my parents did for my brother and me. For most of my childhood we were well integrated into a social system that revolved around political action and intellectual and artistic accomplishment and appreciation. I try to leave my mother's fear and sense of limits behind me: I try even harder not to pass them on to my children. It's hard, because the world has grown more dangerous, especially for women and girls.

What I see as the main difference between my brother's childraising and my parents' has less to do with feminism than with the end of the McCarthy era. My niece was raised in a more open time, when certain left and certain feminist attitudes had achieved the illusion of mainstream acceptability. My niece was never taught, as my brother and I were, to be cagey about the scope and compass of her political beliefs: the more blatant, flamboyant, and vivacious she was about her beliefs, the better her parents liked it. She had a freedom of mobility beyond what even my brother knew (and his was much greater than mine—since my mother didn't identify with him so strongly and didn't project her fears onto him so strongly). It was a point of principle for her to celebrate and facilitate her emerging sexuality.

My oldest child is almost ten years younger than my niece. I find myself fighting a rearguard action to protect my children's fragile rights in school. The issues of race and class are very subtle in our quasi-Bohemian community, but they need to be explicated just the same. In times of objectively greater physical dangers for children, I struggle with ways to enhance their freedom of movement while still keeping them safe. Even in the atmosphere of repression and narrowmindedness which permeates our country, I won't return to teaching my children to hide their true beliefs. By telling them the history of our century I hope to prepare them well enough.

Both my grandmothers worked for the State of California. When they married, they took their husbands' names for social use and kept their own for their professional use. My grandmothers dressed very formally and simply. They cultivated delicately-balanced manners, to convey their seriousness as scientists in a world where women scientists were rare (though not so rare as they were to become in the next generation), and also to avoid giving any impression they meant to challenge or take advantage of the rules about their sex. They wore lipstick and smoked to show they were modern women.

They raised their children to know all the correct forms of behavior. My mother always dressed in clothes from the big department stores in the City, wore heels, and a full complement of makeup. But her glasses, even in the rhinestone cat's-eye days of the fifties, were big squarish engineer's glasses, made of maroon-painted metal. They lasted forever.

Although—or maybe because—my mother had been somewhat fast as a girl, she shuddered at every interest I had in boys, every expression of cultural femininity I hesitantly tried on. She was occasionally exasperated by the more extreme expressions of my tomboy ways, but in general I think she was relieved by them, because they somehow neutered me, keeping me safe from the dangers she saw in femininity: the vulnerability to men's desires, men's violence, men's needs for service and attention, men's jealousy of their privilege and power.

So I was a jeans-wearing girl, and I didn't figure out how to wear a bra till I weaned my first child. It was an eye-opener each time I figured out a new aspect of the deportment and behavior expected of women (don't let your knees flop out to the sides when you sit; don't sit on the sidewalk; don't stand around on corners watching the traffic).

My mother always seemed surprised that I hadn't learned those things and was embarrassed for me, but she was even more uncomfortable when I looked in the mirror or had an opinion of the clothes I wanted to wear.

My own daughter loves the color pink, and lace, and ruffles, and anything shiny. Her preference for the pretty and feminine was articulated before I had a chance to impose on her my vision of a little girl in sturdy shoes, overalls, and Pippi Longstocking pigtails. It never occurs to her that she might have to choose between girlishness and power. She expects to be able to do anything she sets her mind to, including her wish to be a sexual person, a beautiful person.

For my grandmothers, the expression of their femininity was a delicate balance to allow them the freedom to be intellectuals without incurring the consequences of being freaks. For my mother, it was another balance: she claimed her sexual being, but it quite frankly terrified her. I never "got" it, never wanted it, never aspired to it, except in rare fits and starts. Now I have a daughter for whom it is a separate issue from all other things, for whom lipstick and lace have nothing whatever to do with muscle power and intellect.

Does this mean we have achieved in my daughter's generation the empowerment and freedom of choice we have been struggling for so long?

No. It means my daughter will wear little pink dresses to the same demonstrations to which I wore jeans and running shoes, to which my mother wore sensible flats and my grandmothers wore cloches.

Ardena Shankar

Mamawoman

Ardena Shankar

Wait a minute, I've got something to say.

First of all, I ain't all of ya'll's mama, so you can just forget that.

I've got two children, Jamilah and LeRoy.
I named him after his father.
That's the last favor I'll do for that guy.
We didn't get along.

I'm Jamilah and LeRoy's Mamawoman.

She this here, that's me flying over the projects, over all that junk in the street and all those livin' dead folks down there. There I am bringing the groceries home with no hassles. Look, there, that's Jamilah and LeRoy looking out the window waving at me.

Jamilah is very talented and smart.
And so is LeRoy of course!
But that girl is a real artist.
She made this card herself, see.
She drew this blue outfit for me with the word MAMAWOMAN written on it.

'Mamawoman'
Jamilah and LeRoy started calling me that after I had to knock a young man in the head because he tried to take my purse.

The kids and I were walking home from the food stamp office when these two young guys come walking up behind me and tried to snatch my purse.

Jamilah and LeRoy just stood there like they were frozen
to the ground. They were too small to help anyhow.

But I just flipped! I grabbed one of those guys before he
could get away and started beating him with my bare
hands.

I didn't even think about
what I was doing.
All I could think about was
that they were trying to take food
from me and my kids.

I threw that dude on the ground
and before he knew what was happenin'
I was kickin' his butt, his head
and everything else I could kick.

Then Jamilah and LeRoy was
pickin' up rocks for me to hit him with,
and jumpin' up and down and hollerin'
"Get 'em mama, git 'em."

I mean rock and feet were flyin' at that fool.
And he was pleadin' "I'm sorry ma'am I'm sorry!
I swear to god I'm sorry."

And I was kickin' and preachin'.

"Are you a fool! Tryin' to take food from my children?
Don't you know I'm just as poor as you with two children
to feed?
You should be ashamed of yourself!"

When I saw blood on his hands
I realized I was really hurtin' the guy.

So I kicked him in the butt one more time
And I told him to get the hell out of there

And that he was lucky I didn't shoot him.

I had to tell LeRoy
a hundred times after that that I was bluffing
that I just said that to scare the guy.
I don't really have a gun.

Anyhow, the kids started callin' me Mamawoman after
that.
They told all the kids in the neighborhood
and talked about it for weeks.

I want them to fight for themselves
when they have to
cause nobody out in that mean world
is goin' to love 'em like their mama.

So I teach them to be strong in
mind and body
like my mama taught me.

For Daughters

"From a girl's first contact with the outside world—from television and child care through her contacts with peer culture and school—she needs an ally to join her as she enters patriarchy."

—from *Mother Daughter Revolution*

The Lizard Man

Suzanne Tingley

What he was selling was a lizard on a stick. It was foam rubber in shades of orange and chartreuse and it hung from the stick on a string, like a fish on a bamboo pole. It was this year's hot novelty at the county fair.

We walked past him, my teenaged daughter and I, and as we did, he cast the stick like a fly rod to make the lizard jump on my daughter's legs.

Rebecca whirled on him in time to catch the stupid, sensual grin on his face. She was furious.

"You get away from me!" she said loudly. "What's the matter with you?"

People stopped, the lively flow of midway traffic suddenly interrupted.

The grin vanished. "Hey, I'm just tryin' to sell these things," he protested.

My daughter was relentless. She backed away from him in disgust, enlarging the circle of spectators. "You have no right to touch me," she told him loudly.

He slouched away, muttering. There were too many people looking at him now, wondering what exactly he had done. He looked as if he probably wondered too.

Rebecca shook her head and with a sigh of irritation, dismissed him from her life. We continued down the midway, and I smiled at this young woman I had raised who thought nothing of confronting a harasser head on. Rebecca wasn't one to quibble about what constituted harassment: she knew it when she saw it, and she had called him on it.

This generation of young women clearly has an advantage over the last. At Rebecca's age, I probably would have shivered and edged away from the man, blaming myself for getting too close to him.

Lizard Men were a lot more sure of themselves twenty years ago. The high school teacher who massaged the girls' shoulders during class, the construction workers who made loud and obscene observations to one another when a woman walked by, men who gave waitresses a hard time—most were fairly secure that they could behave this way with impunity.

Like many of my generation, I believed they could too. I thought that putting up with Lizard Men was part of life. You ignored them, you were embarrassed by them, you wished they would go away and leave you alone. But you didn't confront them. Like it or not, men had certain privileges.

It was a lesson I learned by watching my mother and by noting how the rules were different for my brother and me. My brother was only a year ahead of me in school; but from the beginning, I had the responsibility and he had the freedom. I cooked and did dishes; he showed up for dinner. I took care of my sister; he hung out with his friends. My father drove me where I needed to go; he had his own car. I was home by midnight; he stayed out until the early morning hours. I do not remember objecting to the inherent unfairness of this arrangement; he was, after all, the boy.

My brother was the first in the family to go to college, and I couldn't wait to go too (I had the grades, but my brother had "potential"). I joined him at the state university a year later. I loved the dorm, the classes, the freedom from home responsibilities—the whole academic environment.

I was on full scholarship; my brother was on academic probation. However, given our family history, it seemed to him well within his prerogative to make a suggestion to me one Saturday afternoon as I was ironing his shirts in his apartment. "You know," he said, "Mom and Dad are having a hard time with the two of us in college. I was thinking that you should drop out and get a job, and help them out. Then I'll help you through when I graduate if you're not married and you still want to go."

It was, as they say, a defining moment. I remember that yellow and white kitchen, the grey ironing board, the blue oxford cloth shirt that needed to be dampened and starched. And I remember my shock of recognition of the way things really were. Go back home? Work at the ice cream store again? Give up my scholarship? My hands were shaking as I scorched the cuff. "Not a chance," I said. And things were never the same afterwards.

I began to take on the Lizard Men one by one, mainly for my own survival. Many of the Lizard Men of my college and of my professional life later were neither obvious nor crude, but their subtlety was insidious. There was, for example, the professor who discouraged me from getting a doctorate because "it's tougher for a woman." Later on there was the mentor at my first job who supported me only until I became adept at my work.

After my daughters were born, however, I realized that sometimes when I took on a Lizard Man, I had an audience. Two little girls overheard my discussion with their soccer coach who had accused the children of "playing like a bunch of girls." Two elementary schoolgirls listened to me question their school librarian about her habit of dividing new books into "boys' books and girls' books." Two adolescents watched me refuse to buy a car from the salesman who spoke only to my husband.

We teach by example. My daughters don't have to know how even today my heart pounds every time I confront another Lizard Man. I am, after all, still in part my mother's daughter.

But they are mine.

Compliance

Deborah Shouse

I am late for the party celebrating Barbara's pregnancy. As I gather my purse and retrieve my black shoes from under the sofa, I trip over my daughter Jessica's parade of *Rolling Stone* magazines and U-2 cassettes.

"I've asked you three times to keep the living room clean," I remind her.

"I read in *Sassy* that nagging increases your stress level," she mumbles, brushing a strand of orange hair from her eyes.

My stress level balloons as I follow a trail of dirty socks and stumble over a volleyball concealed by a moldy-looking gymsuit.

"Sarah," I command, "pick up these dirty clothes."

"When I finish this picture," she says, not looking up from the smear of chalk and drip of paint.

On the drive over to Barbara's I dream of her child-free haven. Breakables on every table top, classical music on every stereo. No Hawaiian Punch in the refrigerator. No Cheese Balls in the pantry. *Architectural Digest* and *Gourmet* in the magazine holder instead of *Highlight* and *Seventeen* on the floors.

I breathe in her living room, appreciating the gentle murmur of adults, the orchestration of Bach inventions, the elegant clarity of crystal wine goblets.

"We've decided what qualities we want our child to have," her husband Ted informs me, as I settle on the unstained ivory sofa. He stretches in his director's chair. In his turquoise sweater, white duck slacks, turquoise socks and gleaming loafers, he looks like a *New Yorker* ad.

"Beauty, intelligence and wit," I guess.

He shakes his head. "Compliance. Compliance is the most important quality."

I remember imagining how I wanted my daughters to be. They would possess beauty, not too obvious, not too ordinary. An intellect that dazzled. An artistic creativity that bewildered and amazed. A sense of humor. These were the attributes I hoped for. These were the attributes I got.

"Compliant people aren't necessarily creative," I say, licking artichoke dip from my fingers.

"As long as she minds," Ted intones, sipping his wine, eating his brie.

I reach for the caviar and try to recall a situation where either Jessica or Sarah was compliant.

From earliest childhood, they shook their fists, kicked their legs, and over-voiced their opinion.

Jessica's first word was NO. Sarah's ME. Every toy, doll, book that needed picking up, every nutritional food, every bed that needed making, raised my daughters' dander, irritated their esteem, disturbed their creative flow.

"Yes, I can envision it now," Ted continues, as Barbara replenishes the ramaki and refills his wine glass. "Pleasant evenings together, our daughter reading quietly, while I watch basketball. Occasionally, I'll indulge her in a game of chess. I'm really looking forward to fatherhood."

"We believe children will enhance rather than disrupt our lifestyle," Barbara says, placing a manicured hand on Ted's knee.

My smile hovers too near laughter.

I drink my pure spring water and imagine Ted dandling a pink clean baby on his knee, his white trousers free of spinach puree and strained apricots. Barbara, picturesque in her Laura Ashley, would cross-stitch in maternal splendor.

If only I'd considered compliance, I muse. I imagine telling Jessica to clean up her room and her saying, "Certainly, mother. Shall I vacuum the living room also?" I picture telling Sarah to collect her dirty clothes. "How could I have been so remiss," she'd sigh, "Shall I do a load of towels for you, dearest Mum?"

As Barbara discusses progressive nursery schools, macrobiotic baby foods and proactive potty training, I suddenly feel quite homesick.

The brie is delicious but I am full. I hug Barbara good-bye. I fumble in my purse and find a damp yellow Lifesaver, one California raisin and a broken friendship bracelet before I find the keys.

I open the kitchen door gingerly, expecting the usual barricade of socks, Barbies and schoolbooks. But the door opens easily. The kitchen is clean. Not exactly gleaming but relatively clutter-free. The living room looks as if it belongs to a maiden aunt. I am panic-stricken. They've either been kidnapped or run away. I race through the house, calling their names, looking for clues.

Then I glance behind the sofa and see the pile of Jessica's magazines. I open the kitchen cabinet and dirty socks drip out.

"Someone called, but I couldn't understand their name," Sarah says, dragging a Barbie swimming pool behind her in a clothes basket.

"I'm starved," Jessica says. "There's absolutely nothing to eat here."

I know we'll argue about Chinese, Mexican or McDonalds, but for now I don't care. I am proud of these willful creative children.

I too am suddenly hungry. For anything but brie.

For Daughters

Gail Thomas

"Oh, may she live like some green laurel
Rooted in one dear perpetual place."
—William Butler Yeats, "A Prayer for my Daughter"

Pull up your roots
and cultivate wildness,
a hungry vine
spreading runners
across borders.
Tell them you have done
with pruning.
Shake custom from your branches
and seed yourself like ragweed
in tended gardens.
Learn courage
for there is danger
in movement
and this too
you should know.

Heather Natt

Rochelle Natt

Growing Free

Rochelle Natt

I didn't like the way my daughter was making her way through adolescence—a slave to her physical appearance. Her long curly hair was the object of constant sacred ablutions. Each shower—45 minutes of applying conditioners—balsam, camomile, natural and unnatural oils, combing them through, waiting for them to soak in, rinsing them out. A ticking oven timer monitored each phase. Then her outfits, gleaned from her closet, mine, even her father's, were never thrown on, but planned for hours the night before in the ritual dress rehearsal required before every public appearance.

Each reflective surface drew her in to peer at herself. Her shoes never fit her. Shoe stores no longer have just small free-standing mirrors to reveal feet. They now have full-length mirrors too. One glimpse of her full body and she seemed to become hypnotized by the swing of her hair, her hips. It wasn't until we'd already paid for the shoes and brought them home that she'd say, "They don't fit."

Where was the child of poetry? The child of piano etudes? The sculptress of clay figurines? The precocious reader of the classics? What happened to my daughter?

"She'll grow out of it," friends assured me, but I was unwilling to take that risk. A psychologist friend told me about rigorous survival training programs available for teens. After careful research, I chose a few of them to present to my daughter. I cajoled and pleaded with her, but what finally convinced her to sign up for the summer hiking expedition through the Southwest was the projected 2:1 boy to girl ratio.

All her supplies, tent included, had to be carried on her back. I didn't argue when she stuffed in hair conditioners and makeup. Nature took care of that. What didn't melt had to be discarded. There were no showers in the desert and often a two-week stretch between baths.

After the six weeks, when I picked her up at the airport, she strode towards me—bronzed skin, hair wild, body lean and muscular, knees scraped from climbing talus and scree, a goddess awakened to her own power. I blinked back my tears.

During the conversation in the car ride home, I noticed that her New York accent had been softened and that she no longer used "like" several times in one sentence. But what she was saying was even more surprising. She wanted to conserve water, stop using products (makeup included) that had been developed through animal experimentation, recycle as much as possible. At last she could pay attention to something besides her own body. For the rest of the summer, she padded around in Birkenstocks and cut-off jeans, her hair free of mousse, gel, sprays and who knows what else. She wrote in her journal, read books on Native American culture and did photo essays of our neighborhood.

However, as the school year progressed, she was drawn back into her body by her girlfriends who were getting nose jobs, manicures, having their hair straightened or permed. My daughter began wearing what looked to me like stage makeup—different tones of foundation to minimize her nose or heighten her cheekbones. Every day she examined her hair for split ends and painstakingly snipped each one with manicuring shears and took such long showers that once again she steamed the wallpaper off the walls. I was heartbroken, but I controlled myself and said nothing to her about it.

Apparently the lessons she had learned over the summer had not been lost, only submerged. By February she herself began researching wilderness expeditions. This time she chose to go to Alaska.

That summer, her letters home were fascinating. I hung on every word. "We just finished a five-day hike up Chilkoot Trail. The hardest part was when we hit tree line. There was no protection from the biting wind. After having climbed 2500 feet, we took Golden Case, the highest peak. The last mile, still carrying my backpack, I had to get on my hands and knees to inch my way over loose boulders at a forty-five degree angle. The view at the top was supposed to make the climb worth it, but a thick fog rolled in and we couldn't see a thing. The others were disappointed, but I didn't care. I'd conquered the mountain."

She certainly had. By the time she returned home, the change in her was permanent. She decided to get a law degree and go into government in order to help protect the environment. She still loves to dress up and do her hair, but these things no longer control her. All my lectures on the danger of women turning themselves into objects had accomplished nothing. It was the earth that healed her, drawing her into its mirror of lake and sky, vaulting her into a new age of womanhood.

The Godmother Network (excerpt)

Elena Featherston

I'm African American, Latina, Native American, Irish, Nicaraguan, Scottish, Italian. Did I leave anything out? But, I'm Black, right? I'm creamy tan but I'm Black. Karen is creamy tan, but she is Korean. That means she's Yellow, right? This is silly. We just are what we are.
— Alexandria Gomez-Featherston, 1993, age 5

The "godmother network" is an idea playwright Glenda Dickerson shared with me a few years ago. When her teenage daughter was having a difficult time with her "coming of age," Glenda found other women to help her ease the child through it. This is the way of most indigenous, tribal people. I've modified her idea just a bit to fit the needs of children of any age.

Group size can vary, but four to nine women friends works well. Ask each woman if she would consider spending one day a month with the child(ren) in your life. It is imperative that the women be different in age, ethnicity, ableness, place of origin, occupation, first language, etc. Mix it up! This is a cross-cultural stew. Godmothers can be homemakers, scientists, single, educators, secretaries, artists, married, lawyers, welfare moms, grandmothers or unmarried childless women. They should be great people who know how to be with a child, and have the time, energy and heart to share with one.

Through one such group, my granddaughter is learning gardening, music, sewing, Spanish, and an understanding of disability. Her godmothers are an African American writer, a Japanese multicultural curriculum developer, a disabled Filipina crisis counselor and film student, a Latina lawyer, a German/Irish housewife, and an African American chemist turned workshop leader. The Japanese curriculum developer speaks Spanish, the writer gardens, the ex-chemist is a world-class quilter, the housewife loves Mexican art and culture, the disabled filmmaking student is teaching her to bake.

From her visits, Alexandria learns more about human diversity than any book can teach, or any misinformation can destroy. She is exposed to households in which all kinds of people are present. She hears and often participates in conversations about politics, exercise, concerts, broken hearts, current events, science, eco-feminist concerns, human spirituality, and race. She is learning, by example, that individuals can be different and disagree but nevertheless respect one another. These experiences teach self-esteem, self-respect, and respect for others, and they impart a sense of empowerment. She knows people of different races, different ethnicities, different spiritual practices, diverse sexualities, and varying degrees of ableness, which is much better than knowing about them. But difference does not diminish her. It is positive. There are many languages to learn, foods to eat, traditions to know, colors to enjoy, and a whole world to explore. Most importantly, she knows, from experience, that we are, in essence, more alike than not.

She is one of those no longer rare little children who treats adults with respect when they deserve it and challenges them when they do not. Recently, I was enraged about some social injustice or another, I can't remember what it was, but at the time I was spitting fire. Alexandria, age five, said to me quite gently, "I am a peaceful Black woman, Nana. And you are too, right?" Not taking the hint, I replied, "Peace is always my first option, but I do what seems appropriate to the circumstance." Very thoughtfully, looking me straight in the eye, she replied smiling, "Nana, there really is no other option in the end, is there?" Having made her point, she went off to play. I wondered which of her surrogate moms had taught her that.

Power

Alma Luz Villanueva

You come from a line of
healing women: doctoras, brujas.

Doctors, sorceress. Though, actually,
in the Spanish dictionary, brujo is

sorcerer, conjurer, wizard - while
bruja is witch, hag, owl. Ha!

Then owl it shall be. Your great-
grandmother was an owl; your great-

great-grandmother was an owl,
and your mother is a witch,

a hag, and an owl. Witch and hag
has always - in time, only 5,000 years

or so, before that Her magic and
Her beauty shone - meant a woman with

power; your great-great-grand
mother, Isidra, travelled Sonora

healing, and she married five
times, each time a better man;

your great-grandmother, Jesus, married
to a man of god, healed from wild

weeds and flowers picked from
vacant lots in Los Angeles.

Your grandmother, Lydia, heard
the healing music through her finger

tips, but the music burned her:
witch, hag, witch. And I, your

mother, hear the word, healing
me, you, us, and though I burn,

I fly, too: owl, hawk, raven, my
eagle. Hummingbird, sparrow, jay,

mockingbird, snow owl, barn owl,
great-horned owl, pelican, golden

eagle. So, daughter, healer, take my
name: be a witch, a hag, a sorceress.

Take your power and fly like all
the women before you.

Fly Antoinetta Theresa
Villanueva.

                              To Antoinetta, at thirty,
                              upon taking her family
                              name and becoming an R.N.

Coloring

Penny Perkins

"Mama, what's flesh?"

Sholanda was in the kitchen doing the last of the supper dishes, while her six-year old, Ella, was playing in the living room. Sholanda had grown accustomed to the battery of questions every night when she got home from work—some uncanny and uninhibited, some just plain inane. It was as if Ella filed them away during her day's activities with Margo only to let them fly at night when her mama came home.

Sholanda took the inquisition in stride, answering nonchalantly, "It's the stuff that surrounds your bones and holds everything together." She rinsed another dish, pleased with her answer.

"But what's that got to do with coloring?" came the reply.

Sholanda wiped her hands on the dish towel and moved toward the other room. Ella, her only child, was precocious and quick to fathom things children twice her age missed entirely. The girl had piqued her interest.

Sholanda poked her head around the corner, "What are you working on, sweetie?"

"Oh, mostly blues and browns," came the girl's earnest reply. Ella looked up from the pile of coloring books and crayons that were strewn in front of her on the carpet.

"They're my favorites, you know."

"Yes, I know. I've been in your room, remember?" Besides precocious, Ella was stubborn ("She got it from her father," Margo insisted). Sholanda and Margo had had a difficult time getting Ella to sleep in a room that didn't have blue and brown walls. They finally compromised by leaving the walls eggshell and getting Ella a new blue and brown bedspread with matching curtains.

"What's all this talk about flesh and bone?" Sholanda asked as she squatted beside her daughter.

Ella went back to coloring and giggled. "No bones, just flesh."

The child was in the middle of a revisionist masterpiece of Jack and Jill. Jill, whom Ella had shaded in her own light brown colors, was going up the hill surrounded by a red rectangle that Sholanda decided was a sports car. Jack's clothes were colored in, but his skin was not. Ella had colored his pail a dark blue and added a similar bucket to the trunk of Jill's car. Sholanda took in the scene with interest, then returned to her question.

"Okay, smarty-pants, what's all this interest in flesh?" For an unguarded moment, Sholanda feared that Margo had been talking about sexuality and religion again on the phone and Ella had eavesdropped. Margo flattered herself to be an amateur theologian, an avocation Sholanda hadn't been aware of before they moved in together.

But Ella didn't seem confused, just curious. She was rolling her crayons around and trying to read the names of various hues.

"I don't understand all the names. They're not all colors."

It had been a long time since Sholanda perused the names of crayons. But she imagined they could be calling them almost anything these days, if she were to judge by the names of the color of turtlenecks in upscale mail-order catalogues: Wrought Iron, Pink Ice, Drizzle, Smoke, Ecru, Limestone, Moon Dance, Marsh. Sholanda had the hardest time matching up the color swatches with the corresponding label. And, she noted wryly, no matter how many colors the clothes came in, the beautiful bodies modeling them were overwhelmingly a lighter shade of pale.

But now Ella was excited about something, and Sholanda wasn't paying attention.

"Mama! Why can't I read these? I thought you taught me all the colors."

"Well, honey, maybe they invented some new ones since then."

"But I know all of my colors. Here—there's Brown...Blue...Green... Red," Ella was handing her mother the tiny wands as she named them, "But what's this yellow one?"

Sholanda didn't have her reading glasses on. Through a squint and a process of elimination she came up with the answer, "Maize."

"What's Maize?"

"It's another word for corn."

"Oh, I like Maize with lots of butter. Don't I?"

"Yes, you do, sweetie."

"But why are they calling this crayon Corn? Isn't it Yellow?"

"Well, honey, some yellows are darker than other yellows. Different shades, it's called. The color of maize is the name for a darker shade of yellow. Understand?"

Ella nodded yes, but Sholanda wasn't sure she got it. "I bet there are other crayons like that."

"Which ones?"

Sholanda rummaged through the pile picking up possibilities and squinting. "Like this," she said reeling one in from the pile, "Salmon."

Ella snickered at her mother's mistake. "No, that's a fish!"

"Yes, it's a fish, but it's also the color of the fish."

Ella inspected the crayon carefully. "I've never seen a fish that color," she concluded suspiciously.

Sholanda sighed, "Well, sometimes the color of the thing gets confused with the thing itself—even if it's not the right color in the first place."

Ella picked up a crayon from the pile. "Look at this one—this is me." Ella handed her mother the crayon labeled "Black."

"Sweetie," she said slowly, "why do you say that?"

"'Cause Teeny said I'm Black."

"The little boy in 4A?"

Ella ignored the question. "Teeny said I'm Black, but I think I'm more this." Ella handed her mother the Burnt Sienna crayon. "See, he doesn't know his colors at all. He's older than me and I know my colors better."

"Honey," Sholanda said carefully, "sometimes crayon colors aren't the same colors we use to describe other things."

"Like Flesh?" Ella handed Sholanda an anemic crayon. Its label had been peeled back as if Ella had tried to discover what was inside.

"Unbelievable," Sholanda muttered to herself. She couldn't believe they were still making this thing. Nearly four decades into the modern civil rights movement and she still had to explain a puke-colored crayon labeled "Flesh."

"Is that the same kind of flesh you talked about before, mama?"

"No, honey, this flesh is a mixed-up color." Sholanda rolled the crayon between her fingers. In fact, she thought to herself wryly, it's the pasty color caucasians used to think they were before Blacks became "people of color."

Ella took the crayon back from her and picked up another. "See, if I mix Flesh and this one, I get me." She demonstrated.

Sholanda picked up the Ella-colored crayon.

"What color is it?" her daughter asked.

The crayon's name was Bittersweet. Sholanda simply said it was Brown.

"No, mama, *this* one's Brown." And Ella showed her a stick clearly labeled such. "I know my colors better than you *and* Teeny."

"You're right, honey. I made a mistake." Sholanda handed the baton back to her daughter. This is a mother's lot, she thought to herself, handing our daughters the bittersweet lessons of life.

"What color is Margo?"

Sholanda sighed, gave up trying to explain, and searched through the 48 options holding up different shades to her mind's eye. She finally chose two and shaded a small square on Jack's thigh.

"Here, honey, it looks like Margo would be a combination of these two."

"What are they?"

Sholanda squinted again. "Peach and Carnation Pink." She colored in Jack's leg with the two shades and added, "At least most of Margo would be these colors." Sholanda leaned down and whispered, "There are some parts that are even more pale."

Ella giggled and asked, "What parts are those?"

"Parts that don't see the sun much."

"How do you know about those parts?"

Sholanda blushed slightly and scolded, "Honey, if you don't stop asking so many questions, your Box-of-Things-to-Understand-Later is going to be full by the time you reach second grade!"

Sholanda smiled and Ella giggled happily. Sholanda knew Ella was very proud of her Box. It was a cracker tin that Margo had given her to put in things that would be explained to her later, and it sat on the top shelf of her bookcase, a prized location. Sholanda had put in several things already and taken some out—like the alphabet and a map of Africa. To Ella, the box was a measure that she was no longer a baby, but someone who could understand things like her mama and Margo.

Sholanda was thinking about some of the things still in Ella's box—like the baby hanging from a stork's beak, a pair of interlocking woman symbols, and a *New York Times* crossword puzzle (Margo was seriously addicted and insisted Ella should learn about the joys of word games as soon as possible)—when Ella pulled from the bottom of the pile a curious coloring book. It had drawings of a burning bush and a bearded guy in a wrap parting the Red Sea.

"Hey, where did you get that?" Sholanda exclaimed.

Ella answered sheepishly, "Margo gave it to me."

"You know you're supposed to check with me before you use things Margo gives you. Remember?" Sholanda had come home early one day from work not feeling well and walked in on Margo and Ella serving thimbles full of grape juice to a photograph of a bearded man with a halo and twelve posterboard cut-out disciples propped up around the coffee table.

"It was just a game," Margo had explained. "Think of it as a tea party with a history."

86

"Yeah, an oppressive—and sexist—white man's history," Sholanda fumed. "If you're going to ruin her with the Bible, couldn't you have at least conducted a commitment ceremony between Naomi and Ruth? Game or no game, this is my house and Ella is my daughter." Sholanda rarely raised her voice at Margo in front of Ella, but she was too angry to stop now, "I'm her real mother and you are to check these kinds of things with me first." Sholanda had never played that biological card before, and Margo jerked back in surprise and then burst into tears. Ella looked on with wide eyes, as she carefully poured the liquid of the thimble-goblets back into the Welch's grape juice jar. Then she padded quietly out of the room and consoled Margo who had run into the bedroom. Sholanda immediately regretted the entire outburst and swallowed her pride (which is hard to do, she thought, especially when you're right), then went to make amends. On her way down the hallway, Sholanda wondered if Ella didn't secretly enjoy playing the two adults off each other. Surely she was too young for that, wasn't she?

"I know," Ella said contritely, bringing her mother back to the present, "you're my *real* mama." Then she added impetuously, "But Margo lets me have ice cream."

"Oh, she does?" Sholanda smiled in spite of herself, "And what else?"

"Margo said I'm flesh of her flesh. What's that mean?"

It means she's a reckless prevaricator, thought Sholanda with irritation, but she refrained from saying it. She didn't want to give too many mixed messages to a young mind—after all, Sholanda had been stressing the fact lately that they, the three of them, were a unit, a clan, a...

"It means she thinks of you as part of her family."

"But you said Flesh was a crayon, not a family. You're not making any sense!"

"Honey, the same word can mean different things." Ella just gave her a quizzical look, so she continued, "Sometimes, honey, flesh is a color, of sorts, a racist—"

"What's that?"

"Something for your box, apparently. We'll talk about it later. Now, sometimes flesh is an offensive term for a color. Sometimes flesh is a part of your body. And sometimes flesh is another term for family."

Ella examined the crayon in her palm. "Colors can be a lot of things, can't they?"

Sholanda agreed and watched Ella add some Flesh to a shepherd's arm. "Here, honey, give me that crayon. I'll put it in your box of things to understand later."

Ella complied and then turned the page to a young man walking out of the mouth of a whale—she immediately picked up the Salmon crayon and went to work as her mother stood up shaking her head.

Sholanda went to Ella's bedroom, full of midnight and cornflower blues, accented by burnt sienna and bittersweet browns. She opened the Box-of-Things-to-Understand-Later and deposited the crayon. Then she went back to the living room and colored with her daughter, sang her songs, and eventually rocked her to sleep. Afterwards, fixing herself a cup of tea and turning on the late news, Sholanda waited for Margo to return from her shift, so they, too, could go to bed.

There, in their tenuous sanctuary, Sholanda would again try to make things clear—that a couple of lovers with a child they were, that a family of women they were trying to be, but a pair of mothers they were not.

"Interpreting to a little girl or to an adolescent woman the kind of treatment she encounters because she is female, is as necessary as explaining to a nonwhite child reactions based on the color of her skin."

—Adrienne Rich in
Mother Daughter Revolution

Emily Holley, Rebecca Holley, and Maria Bruno.

Giant Steps

Maria Bruno

WITCH: (*Total amazement*): The giant's a woman!
—*Into the Woods*, Stephen Sondheim and James Lapine

"Mother, may I?"
"Take three giant steps."

Due to financial reasons, I live in a sleepy Republican farm town in midwestern Michigan, where Rush Limbaugh and Joey Buttafuocco are positive social icons, where most everyone thinks Anita Hill lied and Hillary Rodham Clinton should have stayed home and baked cookies, where the word "feminism" conjures up images of armed and dangerous Amazons ready to stir-fry testicles for the monthly P.T.A. potluck. As a women's studies professor and a mother of daughters, I always had a difficult time of it, particularly when it came to feminist parenting. My Mondale/Ferraro stickers were often ripped from my bumpers; my Clinton lawn signs were stolen at midnight and tossed willy-nilly into the frog pond; my pro-choice banner was a source of neighborhood angst not seen since those transient Sigma Alpha Epsilons tipped over the MacNamara's cows.

My teenage daughter Rebecca had it worse. First of all, I was simply not like other mothers in the community. I was single, I worked, and I didn't wear polyester. I showed up at school functions in my retro-Stevie Nicks lace and velvet, a floppy hat tilted on top of frizzy curls, my liberal politics displayed openly like Rambo's magazine of silver bullets. Moreover, the whole town knew I had a story published in that radical Ms. magazine in the same issue where Geraldine Ferraro, another woman who should have stayed home and baked cookies, appeared on the cover running for Vice President.

At first I told Rebecca to fight every battle. Her eleventh grade English teacher gave her a D on an essay because the teacher didn't feel Daisy Buchanan in *The Great Gatsby* was an important enough character to analyze. This was the same teacher who believed Nora should never have left Torvald, that Lysistrata overreacted, that Antigone was too stubborn for her own good.

During the oral reports at the year's end, a female student passed out uncooked eggs to each member of the class and cautioned them to hold them closely. She stood at the head of the class wearing a starched white blouse and pleated navy skirt, her blonde bangs sprayed stiff into a sweeping meringue wave. Using the Old Testament as her only source of evidence, she launched a diatribe against premarital sex. "God tells us you'll be punished with herpes and AIDS," she said, pushing her tortoiseshell glasses up on her long nose. "And all you girls will be called whores and fornicators and give birth to Satan's spawn." Rebecca cast a despairing look at the teacher, Mrs. Kudzo, who cradled the egg next to her heart, listening intently.

"Harlots, beware, the Bible says," the student ranted, clutching her egg so tight Rebecca was sure it was hardboiled.

"And what will the boys be?" Rebecca blurted, "just boys?"

Mrs. Kudzo flashed Rebecca a warning grimace.

"Think of this egg as your virginity," the student whispered silkily, swaying slightly behind the podium. "You've held it for this last half hour—isn't it precious to you?"

Frustrated, Rebecca plunged her arm into the aisle, paused momentarily, and dropped the egg. There was a series of hushes and moans, then a palpable silence. All eyes turned to the yellow goo that spread on the green linoleum like a liquid hymen, soon to be lost forever to the janitor's indifferent mop. Mrs. Kudzo carefully set her egg on her desk, moved down the aisle, and lifted Rebecca out of her seat by both shoulders. She moved her out of the classroom, snapping, "You're too headstrong for your own good, Missy." Rebecca could hear some faint applause as she was ushered down to Principal Swears, a former football coach, who punished her by requiring her attendance at school on three Saturday mornings.

After I received a phone call from Mrs. Kudzo and the principal, I decided it might be better if she didn't fight every battle and simply coasted through what was left of high school, got her A's, and enrolled in a liberal institution of higher education where she could really test her feminist values fighting sexual harassment, acquaintance rape, and drunken fraternity men shouting gender epithets from the roofs of their Oxbridge houses.

Of course there were other insults and injuries: the Drivers' Ed teacher who phoned and told me Rebecca was "the worst woman driver on the planet earth"; the American Government teacher who scrawled "FEMINAZI" on the board and defined it as if a renowned philosopher, instead of Limbaugh, had created the category; a male student who told her all the boys had decided she was too smart to go to the prom; and of course, the reading list for the Advanced Placement English exams which included only three women writers out of a total of forty.

Then there was her lead role as the Witch in the musical *Into the Woods*. The story goes that the Witch, a powerful type who could levitate, cast spells, make curses, and even raise Jack and the Beanstalk's cow from the dead, is looking for a way to become beautiful again. No beauty of course, but the witch had real power and a sense of justice and retribution. The witch gets her wish and becomes beautiful again. Predictably, she loses all her power. A slave to the superficial, she has big hair, designer gowns, acrylic nails, and four-inch stiletto heels, and she becomes bored and boring. She longs for the days she could zap a scrotum or save the Kingdom. She laments the plastic values of the mortal folk. In her last solo, she begs, "Give me claws and a hunch/Just away from this bunch..."

Rebecca wanted to play her as multidimensional. She wanted to play her with the feminist implications of the character. She wanted to let the audience know that something was missing when beauty was all the Witch had left; she wanted to empower the character, make her a moral hero.

"A witch is always vicious," her drama instructor argued. "Just snarl and be shrill. That's what a witch does."

"She feels bad here," Rebecca said, pointing to the script. "Couldn't she just react?"

"Witches don't feel sad," he countered. "They're witches. Get it?" He scrunched up his nose and parted his lips to demonstrate the familiar stock character.

Okay, so maybe I did her a real disservice telling her those bedtime stories about witch-burnings and the rounding up of good women to be singled out and executed for midwifery, political activity, independence, and widowhood. Okay, so I might have mentioned that the Inquisitors thought Joan of Arc dressed a tad too masculine, that it was easy to blame a bad corn crop on a woman, that female power threatened a lot of men. And maybe I did give her a quick history of female herbalists and midwives and the co-opting of their work by men in the medical profession. And while other little girls were schooled with *Cinderella* and *Sleeping Beauty*, maybe I was defending the fairytale witches and stepmothers as frustrated career women who needed creative outlets. So by the time she grew to accept this leading role, a role I am convinced she was meant to play, she had read Dworkin and Daly, and she viewed a witch's power as positive, life-affirming, admirable.

"Sondheim made Jack's giant a woman," she said after the first read-through. She sank into the couch removing her heavy black shoes. In fact, everything she wore was black, reminding me of the students they call the "artsies" at my university. I call them the "Perpetually Pale," dressed all in black, with pale skin and tortured purple lips. Often they wear medallions and leather bracelets and Doc Martin Hi-tops and listen to Alternative Music.

"What do you think Sondheim is doing there?" she asked, perplexed. "To me, the Giant is the most powerful and becomes a God of sorts," she paused, waiting to gauge my response. "To me, Sondheim is saying God is a woman."

"Bingo," I said. "Now go play that witch the way you want to play her."

I have to say this anecdote has a happy ending, not like the egg crusade and its three Saturday detentions and four subsequent weeks of phone calls from her heavy-breathing autoshop coterie who had interpreted her egg rebellion as an impassioned plea for free love. Like any good made-for-TV movie, she triumphs at the State Championships, takes superior acting honors, and garners the respect of her drama instructor.

No one asks her to the prom except a Joey Buttafuocco look-alike who is majoring in exhaust systems. She decides not to go.

I can remember Robert Young in "Father Knows Best" kneeling next to his daughter and giving her comforting advice: "Now Kitten, you need to behave, be good…," he'd say wisely in that fifties way where all families were happy, all mothers baked cookies, and cardigan dads had the answer to anything. Never mind that the child actress, whose name escapes me now, grew up to be a substance abuser and was institutionalized for depression and suicidal tendencies. I saw it all on Sally Jessy Raphael. Contemporary feminist parenting implies a conscious effort to prepare our daughters and sons for a world where sexism, racism, and homophobia exist in every institution. The message should be: Don't Coast. You need to be prepared to argue that Daisy Buchanan was a pivotal player in *The Great Gatsby*, that Nora in *The Doll's House* should have left Torvald, that Lysistrata and her followers ended the Peloponnesian Wars, and that Antigone was following her moral conscience. And, most important, you need to argue for more women characters created by women writers represented in high school and college texts. Finally, you need to acknowledge as the Baker and Cinderella do in *Into the Woods*:

> Witches can be right,
> Giants can be good,
> You decide what's right,
> You decide what's good.

Ballet! Touché!

Susan Eisenberg

"You don't really want to do that fluffbottom stuff, do you? Why don't we find you a class in modern or jazz?" *Slight humor. Sarcasm held in check. I had probably slid through. But then I went too far.* "You sure you don't want to sign up for Little League again?"

"Baseball just isn't me, Mom." And we were back to ballet. Last year she'd insisted on baseball and played outfield in a red jersey with the name of a local barroom on the back. There were supposedly four girls on the team of sixteen. But at most practices and games, she was the *only* girl, though her coach always swore that the other girls hadn't dropped out and would definitely be there the next time.

Her statement that baseball really wasn't her didn't convince me. I thought it was probably the way her male teammates kicked each other in the shins while waiting their turn at catching grounders. But whenever I asked, she assured me their behavior was no problem. "They never kick me, Mom. They ignore me." Fourteen years in union construction, often as the only woman on the job site, I didn't find that reassuring.

Seeing that extra bit of room between her and her teammates when they sat on the bench, or watching her warm up alone, rarely invited to join in the casual games of toss before the coach pulled all the kids together for practice, was more unnerving than I'd expected. Watching my daughter face the isolation of crossing gender boundaries—all the armor I'd built up as an electrician in the construction industry dissolved. I felt my hysteria going ballistic.

Sure, there had been some improvement: when I was growing up *no* girls played Little League. However, opening Little League to girls, like including women in the construction industry, has to mean more than allowing a few females past the gate. I'd spent years arguing for the need to move beyond tokenism in the workplace, to change the industry to *include* women. I knew those three other girls would never show. My daughter was the token girl.

Two tradeswomen friends who'd been teaching Zoe how to throw and catch and knew I needed hand-holding, came to her first game. A base hit her first time up at bat! When she struck out, I cried. She was committed and stuck it through the whole season, every game. Each time she came up to bat, the infield moved forward and all the adults held their breath for her.

"But what's wrong with ballet?" she wanted to know.

I went through my long list, beginning first with the fact that in ballet women present themselves as frail, needing to be lifted by a man. "I'll look for something else," I told her.

About a month later Zoe came home from school: "I'm going to take ballet and you don't have to pay for anything or drive me," and waved a flyer at me about CityDance, a program involving the Boston Ballet and the Boston public schools.

"They're auditioning all the third graders at your school, Zoe," I explained after reading the notice, already planning how to cushion her disappointment. "They're not going to pick very many kids."

She looked me dead in the eye. "I want this." She was determined. "I'm going to be chosen." And she was right.

On Friday mornings a bus drives her and a dozen other students back and forth from their school to the Ballet's education center. They've been given leotards, shoes, and professional training. And for every performance at the Wang Center—an enormous old theater recently renovated, complete with gilded angels and concession stands that serve champagne—they each receive a pair of free tickets.

I've now accompanied my daughter to a full season of three-hour-long ballet performances, including *Cinderella* and *Romeo and Juliet*. She sits transfixed—literally at the edge of her chair. I usually take at least one nap, though the naps have grown shorter for each ballet. Afterwards, we talk about costumes, the performance, and sometimes about female bodies and behavior.

In the almost one-hundred-year history of my union local, Zoe was the first child born to a journeyman electrician. Zoe grew up assuming it was absolutely normal for women to be electricians, painters and carpenters. She was surprised and disappointed when she discovered men could be plumbers, too.

Once when she was five and a baby-sitter couldn't come, I had to bring her with me to morning referral at my union hall. She looked up from the coloring books I'd brought, scanned the room packed with men and asked, "Where are the other women?" I realized that I'd never told her that the tradeswomen she saw at our house were a rarity on union job-sites. Since that time I've been more honest with her—and myself—about the emotional cost of going where you're not fully welcome, and tried to convey the importance of including that price in weighing decisions.

For Zoe, baseball was not joyous. It could have been; she liked baseball. But to fight for her place in that world, she'd have to love it. And she didn't. She loves ballet.

Watching her live out that passion and assert her place within an adult world has been...a thrill. I say this as a mother, and as a feminist. I insisted, though, on three simple ground rules:

1) School work has to come first.

2) On Friday mornings, when I brush her hair into a bun, assisted by several dozen bobby pins, I must be shown the same respect as adults at the ballet and be called Ms. Susan.

3) Before leaping into my arms from across the room, she must warn me.

"Poke right here," she commands, pointing to her thigh. She grins as my finger meets the firm wall of muscle. "Does that make you feel better?"

It does.

Rosie's Mom Is a Feminist

Ní Aódagaín

Twice a week, I drive through the mountains of southern Oregon that separate our rural home from the closest city fifty miles away, so that my nine-year-old daughter, Annie, can attend ballet classes. This journey, though long and tiring, has its rewards, for I am often gifted with the musings of my child as we pass through the dark night.

"You know, I think Rosie's mom is a feminist," she says to me from the other side of the car, her tone matter-of-fact and unaffected.

"Why do you say that?" I ask, hoping to mask my surprise and pleasure at her use of the term "feminist," a word often spoken in our home, but, to my knowledge, never before by her.

"Well, I think she's really strong, like Sue Ann."

I probe deeper to understand her reasoning. "So, a feminist is a strong woman?" I query.

She recounts a story told by Rosie's mother.

"When Rosie's mom was a little girl, she saw that one adult in the house did all the cooking, cleaning and washing up, and the other adult came home and got to sit in a chair and read a newspaper. So, Rosie's mom decided that when she grew up, she was going to be the one who got to sit in the chair."

"And besides," she added after a pause, "she just doesn't act like other moms."

"So, is being a feminist a good thing to you?" I ask.

"Yes," she says with a certain thoughtfulness, "yes, I think it is."

The conversation ends. The years of dedicated vigilance over my daughter's education and environment had been rewarded. She knew the word, she knew what it meant, she thought it was a good thing to be a feminist. Hurrah!

I remember that moment of comprehension as a lesbian single mother that I was responsible for the child's view of the world and of her place in it; and that at least until school age, if she were to attend school, I had control over the information she would receive. A scary, liberating thought.

I used every occasion to instill in my daughter the conviction that she had full right to be a complete, integrated person and that physical, emotional and mental strength were virtues to be sought. I wanted her to know that she could do anything she set her mind to and that she was entitled within the parameters of reason to get what she asked for.

This required from me at times a certain detachment. One afternoon, when Annie was two years old, I found her endeavoring to climb up the side of a cabinet that stood five feet off the floor, something twice her size. Relating that to my own 5 ft. 8 in. frame, I realized it was equal to my trying to climb something twelve feet in the air. Yet, she was not afraid, only fiercely determined. Pushing down all my protective instincts, I sat quietly, ready to help if I felt her in danger. Slowly, but without hesitating, she reached the top of the cabinet, which, I quickly understood, had been only one of the many steps on her larger explorations of the kitchen and its contents. I learned from this and other experiences that the best gift I could give my child was the space and time to find her own way.

Conversely, I did not shield my growing daughter from the fact that society as it is presently set up can be a hostile place for girls and women.

My mother sent a collection of puzzles and games showing a girl and a boy in a sailboat. While the boy stood proudly at the helm, brandishing a sword, the girl cowered in the rear, obviously frightened by the menacing crocodile glowering at the side of the boat. "Look, Annie. See what this image says to little girls. Boys are brave, girls are scared." The messages come in subtle and insidious forms.

Early on, in an attempt to redress the balance, I chose to change the gender of the characters in the books I read to her, many times making all of them girls or, at the very least, changing the main characters—inevitably male—to female. Once, when she could read but still listened to me read to her, she looked over my shoulder and said, "That says 'he,' Mom. Why are you saying 'she' instead?"

I seized the opportunity to explain how the main characters who were good, heroic or adventurous usually were male. We then, together, consciously looked for stories with strong female characters. In the end, because we found so few strong heroines, she too chose when reading aloud to change the "he" to "she."

As a mother, I've made certain decisions. The options I have chosen—to live very simply in semi-wilderness, to live outside the mainstream culture without television, to be actively involved in an extended lesbian community—have shaped the first ten years of Annie's life.

From my viewpoint, Annie's education began at the time of her birth. I read to her as soon as she could sit up and introduced colors, numbers and the alphabet by age two. Throughout her early childhood, I saw to it that her environment contained all the necessities for fun-filled learning. By the time she was six, she could read, was practicing writing, had a good grasp of addition and loved anything to do with scissors, glue, crayons and construction paper.

Yet, I did not know if I was ready to take on her "formal" schooling by myself, although it was my preference. My fear was that I could not muster the inordinate amount of energy it would take to meet her desire to learn. After being her sole caregiver for six years, I had a clear understanding of my own limits.

The summer before I would either enroll Annie in first grade or notify the school board that she would be homeschooled, I began a serious relationship with a woman who was as radical a feminist as I. She believed, as I did, that the public school system would do grievous damage to the free-spirited, earth-loving, intelligent child she found at my side. She agreed to participate in Annie's home education and thus the decision was made. Our days would be spent exploring geography, civics, history and even simple economics from a decidedly feminist perspective.

As a result, Annie understands that women like Harriet Tubman, Sojourner Truth, and Susan B. Anthony are important in our nation's history along with George Washington. We take time to explain why Anita Hill is in the news. We admit that though it is very exciting that four more women were elected to the U.S. Senate in 1992, the proportion of women to men in Congress is still alarmingly out of balance. We show her examples of classism, racism and homophobia in literature, in the media, and in society. She understands that these "isms" are hurtful to her family, friends, and to people in general.

The concept of competition, explained in theory as we discuss the changes happening in the former U.S.S.R., becomes painfully real when she joins the local T-ball team and is devastated by the notion that the point of the game is to beat the other team. On the other hand, the ballet classes, which she loves and looks forward to attending each week, teach her the principles of working in a group and give the knowledge that working hard for something you love brings great rewards.

Annie's schooling consists of a good amount of hands-on learning. We turn our garden chores into a biology lesson and the weekly shopping becomes a great place to practice fractions and percentages.

However, most importantly, Annie is given encouragement, support and validation that she is intelligent and capable of handling the challenges of both her ongoing education and her personal life.

Driving along in the darkness that night, I reflected on the many different ways in which Annie has gotten the message that to be a strong woman is a good thing. The women who encompass the lesbian feminist community of southern Oregon are empowered women, women who have dedicated their lives to creating a culture that encourages women to become their best selves. As she grows up among them, they honor her for her accomplishments, giving her praise in our Writer's Group, exclaiming over the results of her annual state-administered test, insisting on writing down the dates of her ballet recital so they can attend.

Whether or not she chooses to become part of this community at some future date is not important. Rather it is her present daily achievements that are applauded, communicating to her how important she is as a young woman, in the here and now.

My actions in raising her came not from books on child development but from a strong instinctual belief in her innate potential. As a feminist, I feel it imperative that my daughter's world contains the message that her dreams, visions and goals matter. If, in order to attain those dreams, she must push against bias or discrimination, I want her to be able to call upon her own personal strength and the collective strength of the women who have gone before her.

Hopefully, her mind and heart will hold the knowledge that to be a woman is to stand with your feet proudly on the ground and your arms stretched out to the stars. I want her to believe that the universe is hers to explore and not to be stopped by those who would tell her differently.

As my child begins to move away from the safety and security of our home and start her own journey, my wish for her is that she will always remember the story of Rosie's mom, that to be a feminist is a good thing. Yes, I think it is.

"Through my mother's writing echoes the question 'What kind of world can we *build* for our children?'...She set out to create a community for me to grow up in, she threw herself wholeheartedly into the planning and governance of my elementary school, and she built and sustained a network of relationships around herself, at once the shelter in which I rested and the matrix of her work and thought..."

—Mary Catherine Bateson,
With A Daughter's Eye

Shirley Powers and children.

Paper of Pins

Shirley Powers

for my daughter

"I'll give to you a paper of pins
cause that's the way the world begins"
No I won't
for pins are not enough
I'll give you a plum tree
an apple tree, shade
to sit under, to stretch
into a lotus, or write a poem
I'll give to you
a small section of California clay
a little box house, bordered
by wilted azaleas, shelved
with old manuscripts
You won't have to move
when he raises the rent
You won't have to marry him
for a roof over your head
You won't have to bear his
children, if you'd rather play
your saxophone
You can name it the
house of Artemis
fill it with women
Your deed, not merely paper
"cause that's the way the
world begins"

Hugh and his daughters, Chicky, age 4, and Sammie, age 2, 1966.

Tribute to a Feminist Father

Maureen Williams

At the memorial service for my husband, which we called a celebration, our pastor Lynn said: "Hugh believed in the women in his life. One of his main goals was to let them be all that they could be, whatever they chose to be." The women in Hugh's life were chiefly myself and our two daughters, Chicky and Sammie. And while we both helped to engender in our daughters a sense of independent, free-spirited womanhood, Hugh was the more devoted parent. Being an independent, free-spirited woman myself, I tended to be distracted from my role as mother by my commitment to a twelve-to-fifteen-hour-a-day job seven days a week in our family business and my active social life besides. Yet Hugh, who also worked in our business, never stinted on his fatherhood. It could be said that mine was the driving force of a natural, inborn feminism that Hugh augmented with a masculine tenderness rare in the early sixties, implementing his role in our joint parenting with instinctive understanding, humor and love.

Long before it was fashionable, Hugh would spend time cuddling our babies, comforting them when they cried, changing diapers and, as they grew, spoon-feeding them. Right from the moment of their births, Hugh was there for me and for them. Both of our daughters were midwife-assisted home-births. When Chicky was born, although the practice of attendant fathers was discouraged in those days, Hugh insisted on being with me. He sat up by the pillows, cradling my head with one arm, his hand in mine, to be squeezed as I went through the pain of bearing down. He whispered endearments and encouragement, while the midwife told me sharply not to make a fuss or scream because my younger unmarried sister was in the next room (implying that the pain of childbirth should be kept secret from a woman until her time came to experience it). For Sammie's birth, Hugh played a crucial role, acting as midwife when my baby was born very fast. The young trainee midwife who was in charge, on being faced with her first birthing, became hysterical. Remembering what he'd learned from watching Chicky being born, Hugh snapped into action, efficiently and tenderly assisting me and doing all that needed to be done. By the time the chief midwife returned, Sammie

107

was swaddled in my arms and we were sipping the champagne Hugh had remembered to put on ice.

I married Hugh when I was 18 and he 19. Within two years, we had Chicky and Sammie. In our hectic life, there was no time to learn about parenting by studying the books. We simply had to jump into it and follow our instincts.

My parents tended to be liberal thinkers in the European tradition. My mother was a strong, domineering woman, busy with running the family catering business, who didn't seem to care about me. Yet by example, she brought out my natural feminism. I've always been aware of myself as a strong, independent woman in charge of my own destiny, never feeling dominated or bettered by men. I've always rejoiced in the fact that I was born female. I always loved, wanted and needed men as a part of my life, but never wanted to *be* a man. My father was something of a nonentity, yet it is he I have to thank for a Keltic ancestry that harks back to an ancient system where women were granted freedom and equality. I also knew my father as a fair-minded man without a trace of racial, class or sexual prejudice. He adored my mother and contentedly allowed her to run his life and ours. So between them, my parents handed me the knowledge that all things are possible for all people, that all people are born with equal potential and are equally acceptable, regardless of race, color, class, gender or sexual orientation.

Hugh's parents were strict Victorian types with all the prejudices of that age. There was nothing remotely feminist in Hugh's upbringing, and yet, in his family of three boys and one girl, a remarkable sexual equality existed purely out of necessity. The household tasks in that family of six were divided without consideration for traditional roles. One brother was assigned to cooking duties, the other to laundry and washing dishes; Hugh, the youngest, was in charge of ironing and setting the table; his sister did the mending and sewing (a big job when clothes were mostly homemade and had to last as long as possible). They all helped out when needed, so Hugh grew up being able to cook, sew and the rest. All of them shared in housecleaning and attending to their vast garden that provided the vegetables that made up the bulk of their diet through the lean years of their childhood.

I'd been taught by my mother about the medicinal, culinary and magical virtues of herbs and vegetables. This gave Chicky and Sammie their sense of Mother Earth. Hugh took the time to show Chicky and Sammie how to prepare a patch of soil, sow seeds and later plant out the seedlings in neat rows, then pull the weeds to give the little plants a chance to flourish, flower and fruit. As they helped him in the garden, Hugh talked about sunlight and rain, earth and sky, about how we are all connected and interdependent, how we need the humble earthworm and the bumblebee for our life and well-being.

With the luscious vegetables that resulted from our joint labors in the center of the dinner table, along with the meat we consumed in shocking abundance in those days, we would talk about any matter under the sun. Our girls had a thousand questions which we answered, sometimes turning to books for help. Hugh got into the habit of reading poetry after the meal. I remember how our girls giggled at first at his mock bardic tones. Yet, as soon as they could read, Chicky and Sammie would stand up on their chairs to take turns in declaiming their choices from A Child's Garden of Verses, the Christopher Robin books or my more sophisticated anthologies (The Rime of the Ancient Mariner was a great favorite). Some of the longer poems the three of them would read together, in unison or alternating voices. It was one of those poems that Chicky and Sammie chose to read in memory of their father at the celebration of his life, fervently wishing, as we all did, that Hugh's deep, modulated voice could still join in.

That's the way Hugh was: a father who played happily with his daughters as if he were a child himself, who taught them to handle sailing boats, how to tie their shoelaces and how to make the complicated knots required of sailors, how to ride their bikes. He had them driving a car by 16. He was supportive in whatever they wanted to do, though they were from the start very different people. Chicky was ever a dreamer, inattentive at school, just about getting by, not compelled to achieve until she became attracted, at the age of 14, by the notion of being a hairdresser. "A hairdresser!" exclaimed Hugh's parents. "What kind of a job is that for a girl from a good family?" Angrily, Hugh told them to keep their snobbish opinions to themselves. Hugh was the only father to be present at her classes to allow her to practice cutting his hair and trimming his beard, even when the haircuts left much to be desired. By the time she was twenty, Chicky had made a name for herself as a hair colorist and achieved financial independence. She went on to win state and national prizes, and continues to earn a good living at her profession.

Sammie was always a high academic achiever, winning scholarships to the best schools. Her great love was horses, and when she was about five, she decided that she wanted to become a vet. When she was thirteen she made this wish known to her headmistress. Sammie is slightly built but a lot stronger than she looks. The headmistress tried to discourage her: "You're far too small to be a vet. Besides, women don't become vets." Hugh and I were incensed that such a view prevailed in the late '70s, especially amongst educators. "Just you go ahead and show her, darling!" Hugh advised. "Always the best way to deal with benighted minds." And so she did. Today, Sammie is a doctor of veterinary medicine who specializes in horses.

The self-confidence and belief in themselves engendered by their father was perhaps never put to greater test or better use than when we came to live in the United States. We were all floundering in one way or another and although we stuck together as a family, there was only so much we could do by way of mutual support because each of us was having trouble. Chicky and Sammie were fourteen and sixteen at the time, and if they had not already had solid grounding in the knowledge, both practical and spiritual, of themselves as strong, independent beings, such a massive upheaval in their teens could have proved disastrous. Hugh's job had brought us here, giving us the opportunity of a better life at a time when Britain was in serious decline. He did what he thought was best for us, yet once here, it quickly became clear to him that this "better life" presented massive problems. Although things worked out for us in the long run, until the day he died, Hugh was never entirely certain that he had in fact done the best thing for his daughters. We deeply regretted that he wasn't able to see Sammie graduate and start her career as a vet or enjoy the lively presence of his first grandchild, Chicky's daughter Briana.

Yet he was there for some of the most poignant moments of our lives. When Chicky fell in love with Lenny, the African-American musician she was to marry, we were both delighted, with Hugh declaring that Lenny was the best thing that ever happened to Chicky. (The second best thing, I said to him later. Having you as a father was the best.) Again, he did battle with his parents on Chicky's behalf, firmly parrying their disapproval. After Hugh died, they met Lenny when he and Chicky went to England to visit. Tearfully, they rang me to say they wished to beg Hugh's pardon. He had been right: Lenny was the best thing that ever happened to Chicky.

And Hugh was there to walk Chicky down the aisle. A wedding photograph shows him arm in arm with his daughter, his neck swollen with lymph nodes that were being treated with radiation: father and daughter smiling the same trembling, brave smile. That was the last time Hugh walked. Within weeks he was in a wheelchair, and then confined to a hospital bed in our dining room. He continued to be a supportive father to his daughters as long as he lived.

If I could have brought Hugh back for just one special occasion it would have been Briana's birth. In this day and age the expectant mother can request the presence of not just the father, but also another close relative. Chicky asked me to be there along with Lenny. In memory, I brought Hugh with me into that birthing room. I watched Lenny sitting up by Chicky's head, holding her hand, coaching her to breathe and bear down as they'd learned at their Lamaze classes, just as Hugh had done at Chicky's birth.

As the first days of Briana's life flowered, we saw that her eyes were blue like Hugh's. Now, 18 months later, she is displaying his wonderful, happy-go-lucky nature. And Lenny, chosen by Chicky purely by following her heart, though so different from Hugh in culture and background, has all the makings of a feminist father. It's no longer so unusual for a man to take care of his children as Lenny does, for he works nights as a musician and Chicky works days at her hair coloring. Seeing Lenny filling the role of house-husband, dressing and feeding Briana, changing her diaper, playing with her, laughing and talking with her, I think of Hugh, of the father-in-law Lenny knew for such a short while, but whom he admired so greatly. And I wonder if some influence is at work here. In making his "best thing that ever happened to Chicky" remark, Hugh was perhaps saying: "This is a man I can help to be the kind of father I strove to be for my daughters."

Martha Courtot and granddaughter Sonia.

To Look into the Eyes of a Female Child

Martha Courtot

I was sure I was going to have a son! It was my first pregnancy, 1964, and everyone had sons first, didn't they? I was twenty-three and thrilled to finally be pregnant in spite of the fact that I wasn't married. I didn't really like little girls. I hadn't liked them much when I was one, why should I like them any better now? Girls were so fussy and prissy.

Thea was born, her eyes shining, ready for the world. By the time I had my third daughter in 1971, I sent out announcements on pink paper with an illustration of a woman's symbol with a tiny baby fist extending the power salute inside it. I also had a ready retort for all those sympathetic looks I received when people learned I had given birth to another girl. The truth was by that time I no longer wanted a son. Raising daughters had been a definite consciousness-raiser.

The first time my oldest daughter opened her eyes and looked at me, I felt challenged to provide her with the kind of life she deserved, the future her intelligence and abilities dictated. For me, it was enough to be trapped in a life I did not want, the life of a housewife, but for my daughter I wanted something different. Her birth was the first step in a journey that would take me away from a life of enslavement, in which I could not make any decisions because I did not realize they were mine to make.

My three daughters and I lived as a traditional nuclear family. Later, I was a single mother with three children in the kind of poverty that so often is the fate of such families. We left a middle-class suburb of New Jersey to invent life anew in the Adirondack Mountains, organizing a retreat for women. Subsequently, one daughter chose to live with her father, another daughter chose to live in a group home in Vermont.

Choice was the key word to my parenting. My middle daughter taught me about the oppression of children and insisted on her rights. I had to let my own fifties-bred ideas of parenting yield to my daughters' various needs. Around us, almost every marriage was ending in divorce. Women were beginning to redefine every aspect of their lives. Both our past and our future life were subject to scrutiny. I knew I could not give my children the kind of stable childhood I had experienced.

I came out of my marriage, and I came out as a lesbian at about the same time. Many lesbians of my generation (I was born in 1941) had followed the easy path to an early marriage and children before they had a chance to explore their sexuality. I can't say how this change of identity affected my children. I never felt and thus never acted as if I were doing anything extraordinary. I believe this helped my children accept me as I was. I gave them a model for their own lives—that is, to be authentic to themselves was more important than maintaining some fictive self more pleasing to the world.

Throughout most of my child-rearing years I maintained a belief that feminist parenting could change my daughters. I firmly believed that my daughters had every chance of coming to adulthood as confident, aware women, believing in their own abilities to succeed. My first two daughters, born in the sixties, heard my voice crooning over and over to them: "You are so pretty, you are so good." My youngest daughter, born in 1971, heard a different message. "You are so strong," I said to her, over and over, as if this might make a difference in her survival.

My daughters are feminists, and every year they grow stronger in their feminism. Yet I don't believe that my parenting saved their lives in the way I had wished. The heavy misogynist socialization they received at school, through the media, in their peer groups, was too much for me to struggle against.

Now my granddaughter is four. She is a fierce, strong child, the child of a strong woman and the grandchild of another. Already she is telling me what boys and girls can do. "Boys don't do that. Girls don't do this." I am patient. One of the benefits of growing old is that one develops a longer view. I remember when my own daughters struggled against my feminist rhetoric. Children feel a strong desire to conform. But I whisper in my granddaughter's ear. I buy her books which have strong female characters. I praise her fierceness.

At her birth, loving women surrounded her. The doctor gave me the knife to cut the cord, and Sonia looked back at me with her one open eye. Suddenly I was taken back, I remembered falling into another infant's look, my firstborn Thea. That falling has made all the difference. I am convinced that to really look into the eyes of a female child is to ignite a passion for justice which cannot be quenched.

Cinderella's Sisters

Barbara Unger

We're wiser now
shed envy for Earthshoes
hoofing it sensibly through life
learning to love
our hunchback toes.

Our step-sister outgrew
the glass slipper
divorced the Prince
became a libber.

Outside our daughters
run barefoot
wild   unfettered

finally free
of fairytales
and vanity

come shoeless and bold
to their lives.

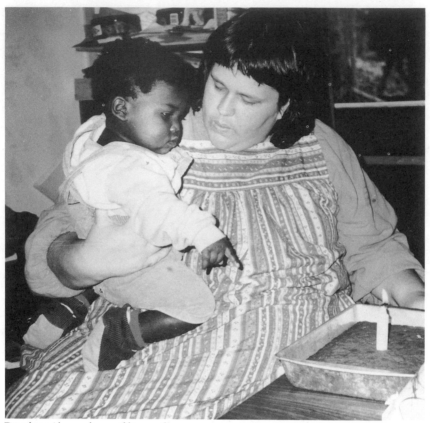

Daughter Alex and one of her mothers.

Strategies for Nonsexist Childraising

Trisha Whitney and Do Mi Stauber

As we prepared to adopt our infant daughter four years ago, we thought long and hard about how to raise her. We wanted Alex to grow up to be independent, caring, assertive, physically active, creative; we wanted her to have a sense of self-esteem that's based on what she does, not on what she looks like or how much like everyone else she is. In an ideal feminist world, each child, boy and girl, would grow up with these qualities, free to be their unique selves.

We have found that raising a free kid is one of the most radical and controversial things we can do. Corporate-influenced children's culture—television, books, movies, toys, clothes—is building an environment of rigid and extreme sex-role stereotypes for our girls and boys. It's *much worse than it was when we were kids.*

Why does the corporate media spend so much time and money drumming sexist assumptions into our heads? A girl dressed in pink all her life ("Stay clean!" "Being pretty is most important!"), shown only books with girls in helpless roles, never encouraged to handle a wrench, will not grow up to be an auto mechanic, an aerospace engineer, or a self-reliant householder. We were convinced that to give our daughter those choices, we would need to take action from the day we knew we were having a child.

The good news is that it's possible! Alex is five now, and we can see that feminist childraising *is* working! Here are some of the areas we've worked on in creating a nonsexist childhood for our daughter.

Our general approach is to look at each possible influence and ask ourselves what message it would give her. If that message is oppressive, we change it if we can, or keep it out of her life. If it's an empowering experience, we use it. We can't change all of society before her childhood is over, but whatever we *can* do will help her to emerge into adulthood stronger and less restricted than we were.

"Oh, She's So Pret-ty!": Clothes

What a child wears helps to form her self-image: how she sees herself, what she can physically do, and how other adults and children treat her. The clothes we feel are appropriate for *any* child are comfortable, weather-appropriate, not constricting, not too susceptible to dirt, bright and varied in color, not designed to emphasize private parts. However, in order to get these clothes, we have to shop in the "boys" section of the store!

One of the most insidious messages given to women in our culture is that appearance is most important. We know a little girl who wouldn't play outside at school because her cotton dress and tights weren't warm enough. She wouldn't zip up her coat because no one would see her pretty dress.

With our daughter, we try to de-emphasize the importance of appearance, while letting her know that she's beautiful just the way she is. We compliment her on what she's *doing*, not on what she's wearing. We don't give her more attention when she's dressed up than when she's in play clothes. We don't present clothes as gifts. Our clothing purchases are not dictated by store labels. We don't compromise at all on Alex's health in choosing clothes, and we tell her how we make those choices.

Once she asked about a woman wearing high heels, and I said, "Those are very hard to walk in and are bad for your feet. It's sad that she feels she has to wear them." Ever afterward she has called them "sad shoes."

We bought Alex something labelled a "Boy's Astronaut Suit." She wears it to school and tells her teacher that she wants to be an astronaut when she grows up. Her big gift request this year was for a space set. If it hadn't occurred to us to look in the "boys" section, we would have missed that chance to open her horizons in this way.

Nearly everyone thinks she's a boy. Our reaction is not to get mad (it's not the most important thing about a person, after all). We've never let these reactions worry us too much. Alex knows that she's a girl, that being a girl means having a vagina and a clitoris and growing up to be a woman. She knows that the people who think only boys have short hair, wear jeans or play ball are sexist and wrong. At four, she commented on the sexism or ignored it. At five it began to bother her a lot. So we decided, with her participation, to let her hair grow long, the easiest way to give people a clue to her gender. This seems to satisfy her.

"Make the Cat in the Hat Be a Girl, Mama."

Books can have a strong influence on a child. If you read to your young child, she will see hundreds of books before she starts to read for herself. Books provide fuel for her imagination. Children assume that the world portrayed in them is the real one. When choosing books, we look for girls as main characters, active, heroic girls and women, nurturing boys and men, racial and cultural diversity, adults in non-stereotypical roles. More books like this have been published recently, but not enough. Most books are about white boys (even animals are almost all male), and perpetuate the same old messages. *Therefore, we change them.* With whiteout, we create the nonsexist books of our dreams.

Sometimes we change a main character from male to female. In Frank Asch's books (*Happy Birthday Moon,* etc.), we made Bear be a girl. So just by changing "he" to "she" and "his" to "her," we've created a book with a strong, adventurous female character. It's also very empowering for the generic bear to be female.

In *Winnie-the-Pooh,* where all of the characters are male except for Kanga (the mother), we simply made Pooh and Tigger into girls (choosing important and powerful characters—not Roo and Piglet!).

Once we've decided on the gender of the hero, we pay attention to other characters too. Sometimes we change the genders of *all* of them. This is the easiest way not to confuse our he's and she's. We just automatically read the opposite gender for each pronoun.

This is a great test to see if a book is sexist. Try switching genders in a children's book and reading it to yourself; if it jolts you, the original version is sexist.

We did this with *The Boxcar Children,* and ended up with sweet Victor (who used to be Violet) fixing the tablecloth with his little sewing kit while his older sister gets a job mowing lawns in town.

Illustrations in picture books sometimes need to be changed in addition to the text. This process also gives us a chance to edit in people of color (colored pencils are useful here) and differently-abled people.

If you try editing, remember to be creative. If necessary, change a whole sentence. Edit violence and racism out. We've even resorted to gluing two irredeemable pages together!

Talking to our child about what we've edited in books and why we did it is a lesson in itself. Alex now chooses for herself which characters to make into girls: usually all of them!

It's Okay to Say No

To give our child healthy, liberating messages about herself and the world, we *do have to say no* to the destructive messages.

People are always telling us, "Good luck trying to keep her out of frilly dresses—you're going to get it from the relatives." It's true that other people—friends as well as relatives—are a big influence on kids, and we've let them know, firmly and from the beginning, what we're trying to do.

The first thing we did was to write a letter in the baby announcements, telling all of our relatives not to send pink, ruffles, lace or guns. Many of them picked up on this (one grandmother gave her screwdrivers this year); some needed repeated reminders, some actively defied our wishes.

We do check presents before she opens them (while she's still young); in this way we weeded out high heels and a makeup kit, given to her for her 3rd birthday. We dyed a fluffy pink sweater bright purple and told the intransigent aunt who sent it what we'd done. It has been hard to say no to our relatives, but it was important for our child's well-being. Not all of our relatives understood, but eventually they complied.

We have decided that it is all right to say no to our child. Prohibiting toys, clothes or activities that we think are harmful is not going to hurt her. By doing this and explaining why, we're telling her that this is important enough to make a big deal about it. And sexism *is* a big deal.

What if she really *wants* a Barbie doll, or unhealthy party shoes? There is a difference between wanting something because she likes it and wanting something because she thinks she's supposed to. Remaining aware of the strong influence of media and peers, we don't assume that every request is coming from her inner self.

If she's wanting something because all of the other girls have it, and we agree to give it to her, we're reinforcing the idea that it's crucial to be like everyone else.

On the positive side, there are *lots* of wonderful toys and activities out there. There are trains and blocks, puppets and sewing kits, red suspenders and African hats. Except when peer pressure rears its head, we don't miss Barbie and My First Makeup Kit at all!

As feminist adults, we decide for ourselves which parts of our culture to embrace and which to reject. We try to base our opinions on information we trust. We know that every TV show, movie, commercial, book and fad is created by someone with their own prejudices.

From the beginning, we've talked to our daughter about what we're doing and pointed out sexism, racism and other oppressions when we see them.

We envision our nonsexist childraising strategies as a way to endow our daughter with her own antisexist force-field, which will fend off the oppressive ideas. It's a kind of immunization. We can already see this happening. At four years old, Alex points to a billboard and says, "That's sexist, because they're showing off her body." If she can say that, she's aware of what the message is and can reject it.

Of course we know that when she is older we *will* be giving her control over these issues—that's part of growing up. We hope that by then her feminist awareness will help her make healthy decisions for herself.

Elayne and Rachel Clift.

The Junior League

Elayne Clift

They're not part of an organized group. They don't demonstrate, gesticulate, or postulate. They simply keep their antennae up and act quietly with conviction. They are, I think, the wave and the hope of the future.

My daughter is one of them—these young feminists who are active, committed, making a difference in society. The point is best made with some examples.

The other day, when I was dressing for an official occasion at my husband's office. "How do I look as *Wife Of*," I asked. "Forget *Wife Of*," my eighteen-year-old, who wears no makeup, said. "You look great as yourself."

Not long ago, while on a singing tour with her fellow students, she observed the dynamics between the husband and wife of her host family. "He sat around watching TV. Then he said, 'Honey, can you iron my shirts? I'll need them when I leave tomorrow.' It was all I could do to keep my mouth shut," she said, jaws clenched.

At a fraternity party, when she passed two beer-guzzling jocks in the frat house, she heard one say to the other, "Hey, man, let's go find us some bitches." She told me, "I turned around, gave them a look, and said, 'Excuuuuse me?' They took off." Pretty impressive stuff considering that she weighs all of 100 pounds and wouldn't even swat a flea.

Or the time a friend said that all she really wanted was to marry her boyfriend and have kids, my daughter said, "Why would anyone work this hard for an education, and besides, why would anybody want to be economically dependent on someone else?" Or the numerous men friends she is gradually educating, lobbying, and enlightening in non-threatening ways that seem to have had a measurable impact on their behavior.

My daughter isn't alone. There's a new generation of young women who give us hope that we will move into the next millennium with significantly reduced machismo. Our daughters may be modifying our style, but they have felt our pain and understood oppression.

They are part of a larger movement which is ebbing and swelling like the ocean's tides. Something is happening out there, something big. The boys know it, and they are scared; that's why they're fighting so hard to deny it and to put women back in what they perceive to be their place. But there is no going back, and they know that too. Women are on the move, in whatever style suits them best, in ways that are powerful and irreversible. It's the kind of groundswell that takes hold when a critical mass is, in the words of Fanny Lou Hamer, "sick and tired of being sick and tired."

Young women like my daughter and her friends are part of that groundswell, and before too long, they will lead it. They will be at the polls and at the podiums, in the classrooms and in the courtrooms, in law schools, medical schools, and business schools all over the country. There will be no stopping them. And then, just watch what happens when some Big Guy tries to harass his wife or secretary, or keep female colleagues on the sidelines, or deny women their due. Without ever knowing what hit them and with no scars to show for it, they will realize that they have been zapped by a female force of warriors who though they speak softly carry a big stick.

I'm proud to know my daughter will be among them, carrying on a tradition refined by her own nature and experience, and reflected in her own inimitable style. She is, after all, the only person I know who can ask a question, make a statement, register a complaint, and dismiss a couple of goons, all at the same time.

Excuse me?

I Am a Feminist

Rachel Clift (daughter of Elayne Clift)

Feminism has always been a big part of my life, but it was not until recently that I was comfortable calling myself a feminist. My mother introduced me to the word and the movement gradually, as she discovered and embraced feminism for herself. However, I did not understand or respect the feminist movement. For many years, I feared the "F" word and felt ambivalent about my mother's dedication to women and women's issues. It was not until recently, after reading works by authors like Bell Hooks and Minnie Bruce Pratt, that I was finally able to understand my confusion and resentment toward my mother and the feminist movement itself. As I got older and more familiar with the movement, I slowly began to understand its significance.

My mother introduced me indirectly to feminism when I was quite young. I was about ten years old when she became depressed and angry over the loss of a job. She felt as though her only accomplishments were that of a wife and mother, and she realized she had creative energy and power she had never expressed before. She began to cry often, talking to my father about feelings I did not understand.

What lifted my mother out of her depression and encouraged her as a writer, I realize now, was feminism. She began going to women's conferences, including the huge one in Nairobi. She went back to school and began working as a consultant for health issues facing women in third-world countries. She pointed out sexism everywhere, all the time it seemed. I felt that feminism had made my mother an angry, outspoken person. Reactions from my father enforced my resentment. "Oh dear, here we go again," he would say with a roll of his eyes and a wink at my mother, as soon as she launched into a complaint about sexism in politics, on TV, or in the workplace. He meant no harm, and I always played along with his jokes; we both felt that it was too much. I realize now how we must have hurt her with our comments.

As someone who now completely advocates feminist issues, it has been a relief for me to realize that I was young, unaware, and steeped in patriarchal values. I saw my mother's commitment to feminism as her acceptance that she, as well as her women friends, were victims. I imagined her women's conferences as places where my mother and her friends would sit in a circle and discuss how they had been mistreated. I felt as though they were angry at being women, so I became afraid of feminism. I did not want to be angry or upset about who I was, and I definitely did not want to accept that I was destined to be a victim for the rest of my life, simply because of my gender.

As I got older and began to recognize sexism in the world around me, I still resisted embracing feminism because I was afraid I would be stereotyped by others. Throughout high school, however, I came to respect the ideology and my mother's dedication to it. I, too, felt it was important to end all forms of sexist oppression. My particular high school undoubtedly played a big role in supporting my growth as a feminist. I attended an all-women school, so none of us felt any competition during the school day. We were required to wear a uniform and felt no pressure about dressing well or looking attractive; we wore the same uniform every day and no one cared! We were encouraged to pursue all of our interests and to be ourselves. Many of my friends in high school were Indian, Sri-Lankan, Asian- and African-American. To be a feminist there was almost inevitable.

Now, in college, I realize that the issues that my mother was facing (and still faces today) really do exist. I, too, face them now. Never before have I been afraid to speak up in class, or to ask a question, or to participate in a political discussion. Never before have I felt stupid for not knowing a fact. Never have I been interrupted so many times in the middle of a conversation with male friends. And I'd never considered myself unusually lucky to have friends from all different backgrounds. Since my arrival at college I have learned much about feminism that I was not aware of before—issues that my mother never discussed with me until recently. I now realize to what extent feminism requires a woman to fight against all forms of oppression, including racism, anti-Semitism, heterosexism, and classism.

I am slowly beginning to learn what the feminist movement has meant to all women in the past and present. I am also beginning to understand what it meant to my mother eight years ago, and what it meant to me at that time. The picture is becoming clearer. I am ready to call myself a feminist, and to join forces with my mother, who has become a source of pride and support as she travels with me on my own road to self-discovery.

"We began to realize that raising a daughter is an extremely political act in this culture. Mothers have been placed in a no-win situation with their daughters: if they teach their daughters simply how to get along in a world that has been shaped by men and male desires, then they betray their daughters' potential. But, if they do not, they leave their daughters adrift in a hostile world without survival strategies...What if mothers and daughters were to join as powerful allies in withstanding the pressures on girls to give up and give in? We smelled the potential for revolution."

—from *Mother Daughter Revolution*

Becky, Anna and Dena Taylor.

Plans with Mice or Men

Dena Taylor

I came to feminism the easy way, growing up in a left-wing, politically active family where all people were considered equal, and fighting for the rights of the underdog was a way of life. I was the first child with two younger brothers and was raised to have absolute confidence in myself and my ability to do what I wanted.

My father taught me how to put together a radio, take apart a clock, throw a ball, and write an essay. Wearing a pair of his welding glasses, I used to sit perched on a stool in our basement, watching him make things out of metal. My parents ordered a book called *The Boy Mechanic* for my brother and me (the second brother was yet unborn) and had both our names engraved on the cover, mine first. This was in the late 1940s when there were *no* books showing girls making and fixing things. That there *should* be, of course, was made much of, and my mother wrote to the publisher about it.

At one point in my young life I was in love with baseball and the San Francisco Seals. My dad and I sat in the bleachers through many a game, discussing every play. And I liked my doll quite a bit too. You could give her a bottle and she peed through a little rubber hole in the small of her back.

My brothers and I grew up in a peaceful atmosphere. The brother with his name on *The Boy Mechanic* would rarely, if ever, fight. Years later, during the Vietnam War, he was the first man to be given conscientious objector status in his county. This was particularly amazing since most conscientious objectors were classified as such because of their religious beliefs, and our family was not religious. But my brother was able to get an unusual number of testimonials from people who had known him since early childhood vouching for his lifelong and genuine pacifism.

My mother was the first and strongest feminist influence in my life. She had every bit as much power in the family as my father. She didn't mince her words, shave her legs, or let anyone put her down. In the days when it was unheard-of, she asked her bank to put her name first, my father's second, on their checks. Even though she worked full-time outside the home and was often busy with political activities, I remember her as being very much there when I was growing up. A strong, laughing woman, she was a girlchild's perfect role model—and because of her I loved being female.

We children learned our lessons well on sexism, racism and politics by listening, asking questions, and trying out our ideas. I can still see us, sitting around the table that my dad made out of a door and wrought-iron legs, serious one minute, laughing the next.

Our parents read the history books we brought home from school and pointed out their errors and omissions. My father gave me Engels to read for an historical perspective on the treatment of women, and my mother came to school demanding the removal of a textbook describing the slaves as leading happy, dancing lives.

My brothers grew up to be quite feminist, very decent men—unusual for our generation. They hang out with feminist women, they promote equality in their workplaces, and when they hear other men make sexist remarks, they speak up. As for myself, I have become an even more radical feminist than my mother (to her joy, I think) and do my best to inculcate my daughters.

In their early years, before their father and I split up, the girls observed us both doing the parenting and housework. Much of the time it was their father who looked after them during the day, their father who shopped and cooked. It worked out better that way, as I was able to bring home a bigger paycheck, and he was a gourmet in the kitchen.

I became a single parent about the time that Becky and Anna were entering puberty, and our lives changed dramatically. We took some deep breaths, stretched, looked at ourselves, and smiled. Over the next few years, we evolved into a very woman-centered and a seriously, if not serious, feminist household. One day when Becky was disappointed because her father failed to call for her as promised, she announced, paraphrasing Robert Burns, "Don't make plans with mice or men." We eventually did allow another male to live with us—a cat.

We always talked: about what was going on in the world, about the work I was doing, about things we saw around us. And the three of us cheered each other on. We decorated the house with streamers and balloons to celebrate each other's triumphs. The girls left post-its of encouragement on my computer, and the day I turned in my first book I came home to a house full of paper chains made from the torn-off edges of computer print-outs of early drafts.

Looking back on raising my daughters, I realize that I very rarely said no to them. I never told them they *had* to eat this or that, and never told them when to go to bed. They grew up with good appetites and thought of going to bed as something nice to do at the end of the day. As young children they were read to voluminously, and as teenagers they'd often pile into my bed and read to me, sending me right to sleep. They teased me unmercifully about how long it took us to finish a book—it was six months for *Fried Green Tomatoes*.

My philosophy was to start with not setting any limits, not saying no, until it seemed necessary, and somehow it rarely did. I gave them power; they didn't have to take it away. I let them make most of their own decisions, but was ready to intervene if I had to. One daughter decided to quit three different preschools because she didn't like them. I saw no reason to force her to go, and I trusted her instinct that they weren't right for her. I supported first one daughter, then the other, in their decision to leave high school early and enroll in a community college. Although I made them aware of the consequences, as I saw them, of their actions, I wanted them to have control of their lives. I wanted them to believe in themselves.

But I was protective, especially of Becky, who uses crutches. I worried about falls and accidents, and gave her more cautionary advice and helping hands than she ever wanted or needed. For a reality check, I'd ask, Would I be saying this, doing this, to Anna, who is in fact younger? Yet even with Anna I was a vigilant parent. When she started driving, I'd ask her to call home every time she arrived at her destination. I taught them everything I knew about being independent, but I watched them fiercely. I don't know how you really let go.

My daughters have told me that I didn't prepare them very well for "the real world," and they're right. Becky, for example, was raised with the idea that she could do anything, that being female or being disabled would not stop her. The fact is, she has had to face many barriers in her life, and although she has not been stopped, she has definitely been slowed down and hurt in her heart.

Anna told me it was a shock to her to realize how selfish and uncaring most people were. She was upset with me that I had let her go off on her own so unprepared. How to teach children to deal with the harshness of life while wanting to surround them with a positive atmosphere is puzzling to me. A friend once jokingly but pointedly told me she was going to take Becky and Anna off for some "sarcasm lessons" since they didn't seem to know what it was.

I believe parenting is too big and too important a job for one person, or even two, to take on by themselves. I am grateful for the friends and family members in our lives who were there not only for the crises and celebrations, but also the many questions, concerns, minor upsets, and great good times.

One of the good times was the ceremony that Becky, Anna, and I had just before the girls moved out on their own. Our emotions were a mixture of excitement (mostly theirs), sadness (mostly mine) and apprehension (all three of us). So we asked some friends to help us through this transition with a celebration. They brought their favorite food, flowers, gifts, a fancy cake, and something that symbolized their relationship with us. Each woman spoke about what the three of us meant to her and told of her own experiences of separation. It was a day that nourished Becky, Anna, and myself and left us with the knowledge that we were not alone.

I consider my daughters to be very feminist young women. Becky once came home from school with menstrual blood on her clothes, and when I commented on it, she said, "Why should we have to hide it?" Anna proved to her theater teacher that there *were* women playwrights in the early 1900s. Both girls are quick to recognize sexism when they see or hear it, and neither one will abide being denied what they want to do because they are female.

Raising Becky and Anna to be feminists came naturally because I was a feminist myself. I supported women's struggles for equality by speaking out and writing about them. I filled the house with feminist books and publications and introduced them to many strong women.

I tried to show them that women could take care of each other, could fix the plumbing, work together, solve problems, fight City Hall, and ask for help when it was needed. I may have gone overboard on the independence part. They hardly ever ask for help.

The Support of Feminists around Me

Becky Taylor (daughter of Dena Taylor)

My sister Anna and I were brought up to believe that nothing was going to stop us from achieving our dreams or our aspirations. By pointing out the unequal treatment of women wherever she saw it, my mother showed me that this is a sexist society and that we should be prepared to stand up to it, and that we must name it as such. Feminism has provided me with a rich sense of who I am. It has been the greatest source of strength throughout my life. I like to think that I have a matrix of feminists behind me. My mother and grandmother are both feminists.

Because my mother could get better-paying jobs than my father, she was the one who worked outside the home. During the day, my father took care of Anna and me. When my mother was home from work, my parents would split the chores up. I grew up thinking that men did housework. Women, on the other hand, were able to earn enough money to support a family and do the work of running a house.

My parents always encouraged Anna and me in whatever interests we had at the time. Over the years, my sister and I were involved in activities such as soccer, tennis, horseback riding, and math contests. My father and I had conversations about numbers and ideas ever since I can remember.

When I was planning to become a computer programmer, I don't remember anything but encouragement. When I brought up the fact that there was a disproportionate number of men in my classes, my mother showed me articles from feminist publications about women in science to let me know that there were prominent women in this field and that they too were concerned about this issue.

I'm glad that no one told me of the brick walls between me and my future. I hadn't realized the effect people's reactions to my cerebral palsy would have on my life. Part of what has shaped me and made my life so full, however, is the element of adversity. The perspective of an outsider is one way to observe what is really going on.

At school, whenever a teacher was having a problem with my disability, my parents arranged a meeting and encouraged me to attend with them and speak for myself. By doing this, they gave me a sense that I would be able to handle the attitudinal barriers and the struggles to come.

About the time that my peers were thinking about becoming involved in relationships, at home I was seeing how damaging a break-up could be to everyone involved, and the relief that came after it was over. I knew life would be better after my parents split up. I saw what was happening to my mother.

After my parents separated, I felt free to start finding out who I was; the pressure was off the household. The three-female house was less tense: we all realized that we could make it and even live well without a male influence in the house. People my mother had known for years started to reappear.

So far, the hardest thing that I've done in my life was to move away from my mother and sister. My sister and I both moved out and went to university at the same time. This separation was hard on my mother and sister as well. We had been living as a threesome for eight years and had a strong network of friends. As well as sharing friends, the three of us like each other's company. We are all supportive of each other and have counted on each another as friends. My own peers as well as my mother's have told me what an unusually good relationship the three of us have.

When I started my menses, my mother was working on her first book, about menstruation. She had been talking to me about the research that she was doing and what she found out about other cultures. On the evening that I started, we had the neighbors over. She told them and we toasted. Later, with the backdrop of the Anita Hill-Clarence Thomas hearings, and my mother editing a book about sexual harassment, our conversations centered on that. But even when she did the books on menopause and older women's sexuality, my mother would discuss the subjects with me. She would show me the essays that had been submitted, and we would talk about them. And with this book on feminist parenting, we discussed and even disagreed on what feminist parenting actually is.

My mother is a great talker who doesn't keep her qualms about anything regarding my sister and me bottled up. She tells us how she's feeling and we talk about it. Talking is a way that works for me to explore an issue and discover how I feel about it.

Often after a day at school, when I shared my feelings of isolation and frustration with my mother, she gave me strength by telling me that no one said it would be easy growing up on the fringe of this male-dominated society. In this culture, people with feminist ideals are often made to feel like no one shares their hopes. My mother urged me to keep going and keep fighting, telling me things would be better when I got older. It isn't just that you have a disability, she said. Women, in general, have a harder time. By sharing these thoughts with me, my mother made me see that what I was going through was a normal part of being treated like a minority. She even gave me a sense of pride that I was carrying on that feminist struggle for a better world.

To Lilith

"Religion, especially the Christian religion, has condemned woman to the life of an inferior, a slave. It has thwarted her nature and fettered her soul..."

—Emma Goldman, 1911

Baptism

Ellen Bass

Her grandfather wants to baptize her,
to sprinkle her head with water
in the name of the Father, the Son, and the Holy Ghost.
He is an old man. He
may die.

Her father wants to compromise, to say
Father, Son, Holy Ghost, and
All That Is Divine. It is
his father.

I am the mother.
I know too much of
fathers, sons, and the ghostly things they have done
in the name of the holy.

I want the water on her head
to be rain. I want her watered as our
earth is watered, to live
in the light of the moon:
the crescent, the full, the waning
cycles that pull tides, that pull sea creatures so deep
that sight is only a myth, cycles that pull
bean sprouts through loose soil,
sap up trees, and plush blood from her womb
many moons from now.

I have no need for the supernatural.
Her breath is the miracle. She
is divine.

He wants her blessed in His name.
I want her blessed in her own.

Rosemary, Maurice and Stephanie Hamington.

A Commencement of Feminist Parenting:
Alternative Religious Rituals of Initiation

Maurice Hamington

May God, the Father and model of all fathers, help these fathers to give good example, so that their children will grow to be mature Christians in all the fullness of Jesus Christ.
— From the Roman Catholic Rite of Baptism

In Catholic grade school there is a theme that is drummed into every child: living Catholic morality is extremely difficult. The Christian life is portrayed as countercultural because of its high moral standards. As Stephanie and I have grown in our feminist sensitivities, it has become abundantly clear that it is much more difficult to be a feminist. The notion that men and women are fundamentally equal is still a socially radical concept.

The initial public event in the life of a child, for those in the Christian tradition, is the baptism (Catholic) or Christening (Protestant). Normally, these are perfunctory social events in the same category as marriages, birthdays or graduations. However, for feminists who are concerned about the misogyny in religious traditions, the routine baptism represents the first potential source of conflict between society and feminist parenting. How can those who are dedicated to justice in the lives of their children let such an important symbolic event go unchallenged?

This was precisely the dilemma that Stephanie and I faced a few months after our daughter was born. We were both raised in very conservative, traditional, Italian, Catholic families. The majority of our extended family lives within a few miles of our house. Our friends were predominantly within the family or from the Church. Everyone was born, attended Sunday mass, went to school, got married and died in the Catholic Church. However, my wife and I had far more education than was usual in our family. Worst yet, we had waited eight years after getting married before having a child!

For many parents who stray from religion, the birth of a child is a wake-up call that brings them back to some form of faith. We underwent an opposite transformation. After years of being disgruntled with Catholicism (fueled by 2 graduate degrees in religion), the birth of Rosemary and more specifically her baptism became an opportunity for Stephanie and me to come out of the closet. We took her birth as a serious calling to end our religious hypocrisy and affirm our feminist values. Although the decision was not easy, we chose to reject our religious tradition. Rosemary would not be baptized.

Officially, the Catholic Church views baptism as a rite which cleanses the recipient from the original sin carried forward by humanity because of the disobedience of Adam and Eve. Modern theologians have difficulty with this conception of baptism and many prefer to describe it as an entree into the community of believers who have the responsibility of aiding in the development of the child.

While not rejecting the value of community, Stephanie and I had serious reservations about baptizing Rosemary into the Catholic community. The feminist issues were many: the sexism of the all-male leadership of the Church; the misogynist history of the Church; and the inconsistent moral theology which rejects contraception and abortion. For these and many other reasons we rejected inclusion in this community for Rosemary at this time. Of course, Rosemary may select a religious tradition at a later point in her life.

In addition, the notion of a baptismal ceremony was itself objectionable. A male priest, who would probably have no role in Rosemary's spiritual development, would have to sanctify the proceedings. It would have to take place in the dark confines of the local church. We wished to remove the ritual from our church and the priest and into a truly sacred place for a child: our home.

We settled on an alternative ritual for Rosemary: an adapted form of the Naming Ceremony found in Rosemary Radford Ruether's (our daughter's namesake) Women—Church: Theology and Practice. This ceremony utilizes common symbols which are in some ways similar to baptism, but without the pomp or involvement of the Church.

The announcement of Rosemary's Naming Ceremony was met by our family with silence. We had debated for a long time prior to deciding to go ahead with an alternative ceremony. In the process we had carefully prepared answers to all the possible objections, but these rebuttals were never used. Arguments we could have dealt with, but silence left us completely frustrated. We could only speculate as to what our family was thinking. This was part of a series of disappointments.

142

The initial disappointment came when the first person we asked to preside at Rosemary's Naming Ceremony declined. Although she was a religious liberal, she felt separation from the Church community was an inappropriate route for us to take. We then asked a progressive biblical scholar to preside and he accepted.

The next disappointment was a phone call Stephanie received on the eve of the ceremony. Her father asked if she was serious about going through with this alternative ritual. Apparently there was still some hope that we would come to our senses. Anger and tears followed this call. It was clear that we had no support for our efforts. The final disappointment came at the ceremony itself when Rosemary's grandparents chose not to participate in the signing of a keepsake book.

Our family and friends gathered on a Saturday afternoon in our backyard. Everyone was reserved. No one knew what to expect. Beforehand, my friends had joked about the ceremony incorporating rings of fire and animal sacrifices. It was actually quite sedate. The ceremony began with an introduction of everyone present so that all knew what their connection was to Rosemary. The first ritual was the lighting of candles with a prayer. Then we explained why we had named Rosemary after feminist theologian Rosemary Radford Ruether. The sponsors were introduced (they are the equivalent of Christian godparents). Together, we pledged to assist in the raising of Rosemary in a community of love. The heart of the ceremony was the reading of the covenant that Stephanie and I had written. This covenant reflects the values we hold as ideal in our parenting of Rosemary:

> We, the parents of Rosemary Hamington, upon her celebration of naming and signing, would like to declare our pledge of the values which will shape our responsibility as parents. These values represent ideals which are an expression of our hopes and dreams, but most of all, an expression of our love for Rosemary. We realize that as parents we will sometimes fail in demonstrating these values, but we hope that this declaration will symbolize the kind of household we wish to foster.

Love and Friendship. This value represents our hope that Rosemary will have many friends and loved ones because it is in loving relationships that people are able to transcend and enrich their lives.

Autonomy. In a world where people often appear to try to control other people's lives, we hope to love Rosemary for who she is and not for what she does so that she can grow to be a strong, independent woman.

Openness to Diversity. We hope to counter sexism, racism and classism by fostering an environment of self-examination where others are not judged negatively because they are different but are celebrated because of their diversity.

Openness to Exploration. Life is too short to get bogged down in daily routine. A spirit of wonder and the ability to risk transforms life from a drudgery to an exciting journey. We hope to give this adventurous spirit to Rosemary.

Peace. We hope that we will model an atmosphere of peace by opposing physical, environmental and psychological violence.

The naming ceremony concluded with a series of symbolic blessings reflective of religious tradition. Rosemary's tongue was anointed with salt as symbolic of the search for truth in speech. Rosemary's head was washed with water to symbolically wash away humanity's history of sexism, racism, classism and violence. Her forehead was anointed with oil as a symbol of courage. Finally a potted tree was brought forth which symbolized the harmony of all living things as a tree of life. Those in attendance were asked to write a message to Rosemary in a keepsake book while they enjoyed a meal together.

Of course Rosemary was oblivious to the proceedings. She had no knowledge of the turmoil. She felt no disappointments. She did not know her parents were feminist or radical. She didn't know she was wearing a second generation baptismal gown. Rosemary was busy doing what babies do—sleeping, eating and crying.

We felt good about our conviction and fortitude. In a sense it drew Stephanie, Rosemary and me closer together. It was a beginning of a long journey that would include many struggles. However, there was a great deal of pain. Our family never speaks of the ceremony or our new religious status. Besides a few understanding friends, no one had praise for the ceremony. It is unclear whether we had any impact on anyone other than ourselves. It would have been extremely easy and comfortable to go through with a Catholic baptism, but it would have violated our consciences. Even Catholic theology teaches that people must follow their informed conscience. There can be no turning back. We have publicly declared our convictions and ultimately we believe we are doing what is best for Rosemary.

It is not easy being feminist.

"The greatest block today in the way of woman's emancipation is the church, the canon law, the Bible and the priesthood."

—Elizabeth Cady Stanton, 1901

E.L. Moore and Lynn Saul.

To Lilith:
Considerations on Women, Men, Children, and Thinking for Yourself

Lynn Saul

"Oppressed Hair Puts a Ceiling on the Brain"

—Alice Walker

It's the wild hair that draws me to you.
Snakes, they say, as they said later of Medusa.
My mother lifts her hand to my forehead, brushes away
the gray waves falling over my eye. Last year, she says,
when your hair was short, it was
so cute. I am forty-five years old but she's hurt
when I tell her I didn't like my hair last year.
I like it now. I like the strength of hair,

power that comes from hair
not being oppressed. Comes from
not having to bother. Comes from saying,
This is who I am. Take it or leave it.

They say you ate your children.
Well, some say I gave mine away.
Of course I never thought their father'd tell them
not to see me. But now they see me, now we talk,
and my daughter, who's shaved off all her hair,
is even more like you than I am.

Well, what it really was
had nothing to do with hair. It's just
that you left Adam, and that worried him
and a lot of other men. My problem, though,
is how hard it is to leave. But I find
that a man who likes my wild hair
I have no need to leave.

Aviva says your opposite is Esther. That's the part of me
I never owned. Oh, I once imagined
I could seduce Khrushchev, who looked like my grandfather,
to end the cold war. But my beautiful sister,
who had straight hair in those days,
was the one dressed as the Queen each Purim.
I was wild-haired Ahasueraus, with a beard.
I didn't know you, Lilith, then. If I had,
you're who I would have been,
if my mother'd let me.

Of course, in the end the point was
you said God's name aloud.
You felt equal not only to Adam,
but to God. On a first-name basis!

Aviva says your revolt is "intrinsically Jewish."
Medusa, Lamashtu, Labartu, archetypal sisters,
did not revolt. Although my mother never thought so

what I wanted my children to learn
was just that: *Revolt* is a Jewish thing.
Lilith, I always hoped my daughter
would be like you!

Lesbianism and Judaism—Finding My Roots

E.L. Moore (daughter of Lynn Saul)

My Jewishness, rooted in Ashkenazi culture, places such importance on marriage, the family, and raising children that women who challenge that norm are often perceived as threatening. Centuries of attacks on Jewish culture and life have made the strengthening of family a very real need. But to make the nuclear family central to Jewish life means that the contributions to Jewish culture and community by lesbians, gay men, single people, and anyone living outside that reality are ignored.

I've heard it too many times: "Have you met any nice Jewish boys at school?" "Did you hear your second-cousin-twice-removed got married? Oh, what a beautiful wedding she had." "When you have children you'll know what I mean." "Erica, I'm just *thrilled* to hear you like to cook." "Why do you want to cut your hair and look unattractive to men? It's so *unfeminine*." My grandmother knows our family tree inside and out. She knows who's married to whom and the names of everyone's children. She accepts my wish not to have children only because my cousin wants to have eight.

It's funny how culture works. The Jewish extended family I grew up in, like the Christian country I live in, taught me to want a husband and children. Yet it is precisely the Jewish women in my family whom I've looked to as sources of strength: My great-grandmother who told me to get an education so I would never have to rely on a man; she who was the focal point for a large extended family; she who lived to be ninety-four, surviving her husband so that in the twenty years I knew her, I saw a woman living alone and independent. My great aunt Tanta Fanny, who ran a business by herself for as long as I can remember. My mother, who chooses to live life as she pleases regardless of other people's judgments; my mother who taught me that social justice is a Jewish thing, that "revolt is a Jewish thing." How could I be other than who I am? How could my love for women be unJewish?

And yet, even on Shabbat, my favorite time to spend with Jewish women friends, I hear that traditional prayer that conceptualizes the presence of the divine in the world, through the union of Shekinah and Tiferet, feminine and masculine aspects of God. How ironic to be welcoming the Shabbos bride and singing wedding songs among women who have taught me to be so critical of the ways marriage is oppressive to women.

Then again, as Jewish lesbians and feminists we can reshape symbols like the Shabbat marriage, creating new meanings and interpreting prayers and images in ways that represent us and our experiences. Shekinah becomes the divine part of ourselves whom we are reunited with on Shabbat, or a Goddess welcomed for herself rather than for her status as bride.

What does it mean if we continue to believe that lesbian Jews don't exist or can't participate in Jewish culture? It means that I cannot identify myself strongly as a Jew. It wasn't until my mom sent me a copy of *The Tribe of Dina* (a Jewish feminist anthology) and I picked up *Nice Jewish Girls* (a lesbian anthology), that I began to feel that I had a place to speak from *as a Jew*. Discovering that there are women committed to integrating their feminist and lesbian politics with their progressive Jewish politics made me excited to be a Jew and to have that strong community and history to draw on and change within.

What about the Boys?

"'Boys will be boys' is said far too often, even by feminists, and the same folks who will crucify you for implying that menstrual cycles affect women's judgment insist that boys' behavior is dictated by their hormones."

—Renee Augrain
in *Blue Stocking*, 4/93

Poison

G. Marault

Jake was about 5 when he went through that phase where he had to punch me in the stomach from time to time. I don't know. To get my attention. To test his boundaries. To have contact with me. To feel big and strong. Or because he'd seen so many men on TV hitting women. For whatever reason, he was in that phase.

We went to my mother's one afternoon, and he started up.
I began by saying,
"Jake. Stop."
He'd just smile at me.
Whack, again, into my tummy.
I held onto his little fist. It was just a challenge to him.
He used the other hand.

In a voice I never heard her use on me, my mother pleaded gingerly,
"Jacob, don't hit Genie. You're a big strong boy and she's just a girl."

Just a girl. JUST A GIRL.
"Jake," I said,
"Gramma's trying to fill your head with poison"
(at which my mother sputtered).
"The reason you shouldn't hit me is because you wouldn't want me to hit you. Would you? I'm twice as big as you and I'd knock you across the room. I love you, though, so I'd never hit you, and it would make me happy if you loved me the same way."

He was probably too busy struggling to free his hands to hear a word I said, but I said it. And I said to my mother,
"What is *just a girl*? What kinda crap is that?"
Like always, she had no answer for me.

Boy Thangs

Kate Luna

"Budi, come on, it's time to go! We're going to be late." In he comes, decked to the teeth—a mixture of Rambo, Ninja Warrior and Pancho Villa. We're on our way to a Stop U.S. Intervention rally and my four-year-old looks like he could take out an entire Nicaraguan village by himself—swords crossed over chest, arrows and a bow in belt, grenade in his pocket, two holsters, a machine gun down his back.

We had a no gun rule at one time. I meant to keep it, but plumbing fittings became grenades and vacuum parts were transformed into rocket launchers. Soon rules seemed futile. I won't buy the stuff. I don't encourage it as gifts from grandparents and favorite uncles, but he manages to acquire arsenals in trade for dinosaur coloring books and sticker collections.

"Budi, are you going to bring all that stuff with you? 'Cause we're taking the bus and I'm not going to carry it for you if you get tired of lugging it all around. You are going to have to be responsible for all of it." We walk to the bus, ammunition clanging and crashing at his sides. People stop on the street to stare at my megawarhead son. "Hi, I'm a pacifist and this is my future Soldier of Fortune son, Budi." Maybe I can think of him as a potential Che or a Sandinista. Channel the gun thang into positive revolutionary aspirations.

"Pow, bam, bam bam bam bam bam, kaboom, crash, crash. Katy (he calls me Katy), if you could pick between an AK47 or an Uzi, what would you pick?"

"Uhhh...um...I don't know, Budi, I don't care about that stuff. I don't want to pick!"

"Just pick, Katy."

"I don't want to."

"Pick!"

"O.K.! An Uzi."

"Yeah, me too."

I wake from a dream one morning and in this dream someone is trying to break into our house and I was trying to hide. I lie awake with my heart pounding. Budi calls out to ask if he can climb into bed with me.

154

Thumb in mouth, curled up, he asks, "Katy, what would you do if a monster came in the room and tried to get me?"

"I would scream at it to 'GET AWAY' and 'don't you dare try to hurt us.'"

"What if it was a guy who tried to kidnap me?"

"I would make myself really big inside and kick and scream and yell and bite."

"What if he had a gun. What would you do? Would you wish you had a gun?"

"Maybe."

"If you had a gun would you use it?"

And I realize that this child of mine is not asking for philosophy—no nonviolent conflict resolution. He needs to know if I would do anything.

Thumb-sucking, prodding, "If someone tried to hurt you, Katy, I would blow his head off!"

"Me, too, Bud. I would blow them to smithereens!"

Later we can discuss alternatives. Right now the world seems too big, too out of control, and his plastic P.V.C., T-joint plumbing handgun a small comfort for this tenderhearted boy and his mama.

A small grin passes over his face as I leap up and take on our imaginary assailant.

"BAM, BAM, BAM, POW, POW," kick, kick, kick, swords flying, grenades launched, arrows sail. MegaMom strikes fear in the heart of kidnappers and relief for a small son.

"Budi, here's a cool book on dolphins. You want to check out this one?"

"No, do you know where the police books are? What about attack dogs?"

"Budi, I don't want you to get a bunch of weapon books, O.K.?"

"But, Katy, they aren't for you. They're for me. It's what I'm interested in. You get to pick the books for you and I get to pick the books for me. That's what's fair."

"But, Budi, you end up filling your mind with all that stuff and it makes up who you are and who you become. Like the food you eat. You're choosing to fill up your consciousness with junk."

"It isn't junk to me, Katy. It's interesting. I like learning about it."

I try setting boundaries: one dolphin book per *Machine Gun Illustrated*; one book about snakes for every *Green Beret Guidebook*. These feeble attempts at balance in an out-of-balance world. I am forced to trust, to believe that there is a solid place in the heart of this young boy. He forces me to trust.

"Budi, it's just that there are so many messages out there for guys that guns and violence are a solution and that it is cool or something. 'Be All You Can Be.' What bullshit! Military is about killing. Killing grandmas and babies and moms and kids and it doesn't fix anything and it freaks me out to think you might believe their trip."

"Katy, you know me. I don't want to hurt anybody. It's just toys and games and stuff that I'm interested in right now, but I don't want to hurt anybody. You know me."

Tears come. "It's just so scary to trust, Bud. They can be so convincing and what if you believe them. What would I do if you got killed in a war? My heart would be broken forever."

"Don't worry, Katy. I'm going to be fine. Do you think they have any books on crossbows?"

"Budi, no, I am not renting *The Terminator*. Forget it. I don't care if you already saw it. Where did you see it? Let's try and find something we both like."

"Sure, Katy, like *Lassie, Come Home* or *Gandhi*? Real fun!"

"Bud, there's got to be something here that we can agree upon. There's 7,000 videos. There's got to be one."

"*Lethal Weapon*?"

"No. How about *Call of the Wild*?"

"Saw it. *New Jack City*?"

"It's an R, Budi. I don't want you seeing a bunch of R-rated movies. You're 11 years old. How come everything's an R? There are no G movies anymore and barely any PG's. Everything's an R!"

"What's wrong with R's, Katy?—just some bad language."

"No, Budi. Look, here's the rating thing. G says 'O.K. for people of all ages. Kids can understand them. Any sexual material is shown in a loving relationship. Any violence is shown as a force of law and order.' Well, I don't know about that as a solution for solving problems. There's always a clear choice between right and wrong. PG—'Kids can understand the big theme, but there can be other themes which are important to the film which younger kids might not understand. It is possible to refer to sex outside of loving relationships, as long as that isn't done for the main characters. More violence is allowed, but it still must follow the guideline in the G films. R—a film with an R rating is based on an adult idea. The idea is one that kids might not understand. The limits on sex and violence and right and wrong do not hold.' I don't like all that violence, and I'm *really* uncomfortable about how they show sexuality. I

156

mean, nobody is tender or sweet and gentle and loving. It's the most casual sex and rape with nobody really deeply caring about each other, and I don't feel like that's O.K. for you. Nobody uses any birth control or condoms. Everybody's taking advantage of everybody else. They meet in a bar and chat for an hour, then they go back to an apartment, take all their clothes off and have sex. That is so weird to me. Nobody's showing any other way. I get really mad because all the women take their clothes off and show everything to a perfect stranger whereas all the men are covered up and none of the women ever weigh more than 125 pounds and have these perfect bodies. All my life I've tried to live up to that. It has been really painful and it's not O.K. with me for you to fill yourself up with that as your idea of sexuality."

My son, who couldn't sit through 101 *Dalmatians* because "that lady is just too mean," covers his eyes when the mother dies in *The Bear*, and cries when the wolf is killed in *Dancing with Wolves*, manages to sit in rapt attention as whole towns are exploded, buses demolished, cars set afire, heads decapitated.

"Budi, how can you stand to watch this?"

"It's good special effects, Katy. It's a movie, not for reals."

We depart Video Madness in an impasse, decide to go home and play rummy, finish the last chapter of *Old Yeller* and call it a night.

"Katy?"

"Yeah, Bud?"

"I love you."

"I love you, too, Bud. So very much."

"Katy, can I get the *Sports Illustrated Swimsuit Edition*?"

Anne Mackenzie and son Tyler.

Just Tyler and Me

Anne Mackenzie

I never expected to raise Tyler alone. I never thought I'd only have just one child either, but here I am, a single mom with a son.

If I'd known that children normally identify with the same sex parent at age four, maybe I would have left Tyler's dad sooner. Or maybe later. No, sooner. Anyway, Tyler was the prime age for same-sex-identification and due to all the things going on during my marriage and my leaving, Tyler decided to reject his dad. And pretty much all men for a while.

And identify with me.

Oops! That's not supposed to happen! That's supposed to happen at a later date or an earlier one or something. That time when little boys think it would be fun to be little girls and little girls think it would be fun to be little boys and vive la différence! Well, Tyler started that one a little early.

It wasn't as if Tyler was a macho little boy in the first place. He wasn't like his cousin Alex who had all of those "boy" things from birth. Alex was always the dare-devil-inarticulate-erector-set-zoom-zoom-wild-boy. I remember holding Alex as an infant and feeling the energy and intensity radiating from him.

Tyler was never like that. He was quieter. He was sweeter. He was more androgynous. Always. Maybe it's astrology, maybe it's karma, but Tyler chose toys and game playing by whatever appealed to him, not by whether it was a boy-thing or a girl-thing to do. Tyler has always been, well, just *Tyler*, himself.

Frankly, I've always been pleased that he is exactly who he is. That's all I've ever wanted him to be. But you can see how it could get to be a little worrisome when our living situation changed so drastically.

When I left Tyler's dad, I took Tyler and a suitcase of clothes for each of us. That's it. My parents were helping me out, but they certainly weren't going to buy me all the minimal household things one needs to get by, like towels, sheets, dishes, pots and pans. So when I went looking for a place to live, I looked to share a house with somebody.

My older sister had a friend who rented out the master bedroom of his house for cheap. It seemed the ideal situation: a ready-made place to live, with a single father of a ten-year-old girl, and he was totally involved with someone. Safe. We moved in.

Living with Dennis and Elsa was great. I still think it was good for all of us as both of the children got to see "platonic parents" interact in a friendly way, without fighting and trauma. Each child had a same-sex adult in the house to model after and Dennis and I had a built-in baby-sitter.

Tyler and Elsa would play together sometimes. Elsa liked to put on "performances" for us and now she had Tyler to sing and dance along with her. Tyler really liked these performances with Elsa, especially because he could twirl around in long swirly skirts.

He saw Elsa playing with fingernail polish and makeup and he wanted to play with it too. It seemed normal to me that he would want to play with these things. I knew boys go through this "stage," and so I let him wear fingernail polish sometimes. But I wondered whether it was the right thing to do because he didn't have a father to model after. Should I tell him "no" about these things? Should I be tougher, insist he do only "macho" boy things? I didn't think that was right either, but I just wasn't sure what I was supposed to do under these circumstances.

You can imagine my dismay when Tyler started telling me he wished he was a girl. Girls got to do all the fun things like makeup and fingernail polish and swirly skirts. Why do girls get to do all the fun things? What do boys get to do?

Tough question! Aside from the obvious advantages like higher pay, more job advancement and physical strength, what were the good things about being a boy? I decided to ask my liberal men-friends that question.

All of the men I asked said, "Gee, I don't know," but somehow I got the feeling they were trying to be politically correct. It still left the answer up to me.

So I told Tyler the truth. I told him that one day he would be bigger and stronger than me and that he could pee anywhere he wanted without getting his socks wet.

Tyler loved the part about being bigger and stronger than me. He is now twelve and compares his height almost daily to mine (he is still shorter). But the part about being able to pee anywhere he immediately put into practice.

I am a night owl and whenever possible, I sleep in in the morning. Living with Dennis and Elsa enabled me to indulge my late night habits. One day, Dennis nonchalantly asked if I knew that Tyler was going out every morning and peeing on the tree in front of the house.

"Uh, no," I said. "Every morning?"

160

"Yep," Dennis replied, "every morning."

Needless to say, I had a little chat with Tyler about this. I promised myself to remember that Tyler always takes me literally.

All of this left me unprepared for an evening some time later when Tyler sashayed his way to the kitchen wearing a wig, headband, makeup, swirly skirt with slips under it, jewelry, and high heels. In a little girl voice and a swish of his hand he said, "Hi mommie, don't I look pretty?"

Turning to Dennis, I whispered, "There he is, a single mother's nightmare."

He isn't, I know. He's just *Tyler* and this is all just part of growing up, but I tell you, it's hard when you're a single mom raising a boy.

I noticed that Dennis, a single dad raising a girl, was a little bit more feminine than some other men I knew. He does the dishes and cleans the counters and does the laundry; all of these things are perfectly normal for any parent raising any child but when there are two parents around, in general, men don't even see the counters are dirty, let alone clean them. Dennis is actually a '90s woman's dream come true and, believe me, all the women know it.

We talked one time about how, as single parents of an opposite sex child, we took on the traits of that sex to try to give our children a more rounded role model. We consciously chose to develop these traits, whether our personalities were actually that way or not.

I know that I had to develop a whole different attitude about bugs. I hate bugs. I hate spiders especially because they have so many little legs that tickle when they crawl on you. I generally go through the usual "woman" routine making all the "oohhh" noises and being rather squeamish around spiders. At least, I used to.

Now, John Wayne has nothing on me, pilgrim. Shoot, I can track 'em down and squish 'em without battin' an eye and all the while saying, "Tyler, don't be so scared, it's just a spider and there! It's dead now! See? Nothing to be scared of, we got 'im."

Until he goes to bed.

THEN I do all my "oooohhhs" and "yuks" and dance around waving my arms shivering and saying over and over, "I HATE spiders! I HATE spiders!" But only when Tyler's asleep. During the day, I am brave and strong and fearless for I have a son and I must embody the masculine traits for him to model after. But nobody said it was easy.

I am no longer the woman I thought I would be—not in appearance or style. I am someone I never dreamed I would end up being, largely because I am a single mother of a son.

As it is with all parents, there were choices I had to make along the way. Directions I had to go so that my son would have influences that I felt were better for him. I would choose them again. I have no qualms about the choices I made. I'm just surprised to be this big, tough woman alone at 43.

But my son knows I love him, that he is loved and loveable. My son is secure in his place in the world and in himself. He knows that who he is is okay.

And that's all that matters. Really.

The Barbie Liberation Organization, made up of parents, feminists and other activists, says it switched the voice boxes on 300 GI Joe and Barbie dolls during the 1993 Christmas season. In a high-pitched voice, Joe stands at the ready, machine gun and hand grenades at his side, saying, "Want to go shopping? I love school, don't you?" Barbie, in a deep voice, says, "Dead men tell no lies." "Our goal is to reveal and correct the problem of gender-based stereotyping in children's toys," says the BLO. An 8-year-old who received an altered GI Joe from his grandparents said, "I love him." "I'm really happy it worked out this way," said the boy's mother. "Our job is to help him understand so that he doesn't think he has to be a soldier."

—from AP, 12/29/93

Joan Joffe Hall and son,1967.

Matthew at Thirteen

Joan Joffe Hall

My son is looking for the right
length of string. He has a big ball
of string ends that he gives me
to hold loosely while he pulls
gently at an end, walking away.
One after another, a dozen
or more strips come loose,
none quite long enough—
his height—for the game
underway in his room.

I've always admired
women with grown sons,
and wondered how a boy's body
finds its size

            I made
some off-color joke
and laughing he reproved me:
didn't I know mothers
shouldn't carry on like that?
and would I please
not do it in front of his friends.

He told one boy in a fight
about abortion just to imagine
being thirteen, female, raped
and pregnant. The kid refused,
said it couldn't happen to him.
Then don't talk, my son said.

When I call him on the phone
I know I'm hearing my own voice.
When he first got braces
I put my fingers in my soft mouth;
his eyes are mine, his bad skin too.
But also they are his;
and the body lengthens
and hardens, pulls away.

Raising Sons

Robin Morgan

"It's a boy!"

Depending on the culture you live in, your life may now be worth something. You might not be shamed, beaten, or divorced; your husband might not take a second wife; you might not starve in your old age.

Depending on the culture you live in, you are now a stereotype: a possessive "Jewish mother" or castrating "black matriarch"; devouring, manipulative, self-martyring, guilt-provoking; pilloried by Sigmund Freud, demonized by Philip Roth.

Whoever and wherever you are, if you are a feminist, the words "It's a boy" preface one of the greatest challenges you'll ever know.

As feminists, we've focused on mothers and daughters—understandably, since whether or not we're mothers, all women are daughters. But can we avoid The Other Touchy Subject? The personal *is* political.

So we've wrung our hands and hearts, comparing notes in hundreds of quiet conversations. I remember one talk with a grass-roots activist in a Midwest urban slum neighborhood—a courageous African American woman who confronted drug pushers daily without flinching, but confessed her greatest fear was that, in laying down strict rules for her young son to protect him, she would someday taste his bitter accusations that she'd robbed him of his "manhood." I recall another conversation with a European woman of inherited wealth who had turned her largesse into philanthropy for women, who worried that despite her teaching and example her sons might become playboys once they came into their trust funds. And I'll never forget the exchange with an advocate for battered women, herself a battery survivor in her late fifties, who wept that years earlier she had been unable to get her son "away from him in time"—and added, in answer to my unasked question, "Every rapist is some mother's son."

We've watched many women indulge their sons in ways they never would their daughters. We've watched some preach one way and practice another. We've watched women refuse to "inflict" the insights of feminism on their sons out of homophobic ignorance and terror that a sensitive male will turn out "effeminate" or gay (so what if he does?).

167

We've watched women boast of their ideal "feminist" sons, creating a future Feminist Prince problem. (You know, the guy who gobbles up the latest copy of Ms. before his wife has time to glance at it, and then pontificates on tactics "you women ought to be using.") We've even watched some women crush their sons' spirits in the name of militant politics.

Parenting—in truth, given the realities, mothering—a child of either sex is a major job. Society claims to revere it but is rarely supportive, and then only when the mother is not a lesbian, or employed outside the home, or trying to survive on welfare. Meanwhile, we confront internal contradictions: we want our children to be themselves, not extensions of ourselves, to make their own decisions, and *also* to reject the patriarchal status quo.

The challenges faced by a feminist rearing a daughter are enormous—but at least you can tell her, without ambivalence, "Go for it! Don't let anyone stop you!" With a son, you must somehow erode the allure of male entitlement and communicate a delicate double message: "Fulfill yourself to the utmost as a human being—but try to divest yourself of the male power that routinely accrues to you. Be all you can as a person—but don't forget your automatic male advantages are bought at a cost to female people." If, as in my case, the son is European American, you try to communicate a comparable message about being white in a racist culture.

And all this takes place under a propaganda barrage that makes Schwarzkopf/Schwarzenegger values seem normal.

Blake Morgan, born ten days before humans first walked on the moon, is now 24 years old. He is an artist I respect, a companion I enjoy, a friend I cherish. He has a sense of humor and a sense of justice, a damned good combination (and one that allows me to gloat retroactively at all those people who were certain a feminist's son would grow into a twitching neurotic). What's more, he makes a great garlic-tomato sauce for his perfectly timed pasta. He is the only man I truly love.

Like any woman, I can speak only from my experience. I offer it trusting that whenever women dare name our truths, failures and triumphs to one another, we all benefit.

Blake was a wanted, and an only, child. His father, the poet and writer Kenneth Pitchford, and I were both fortunate to earn our livelihoods by work we chose and loved: writing books, augmented by freelance editing. The financial insecurity was a trade-off for the luxury of having time—to do one's own work and to be with Blake. Not everybody has such choices.

Here the issue of men and child care is again important; I wasn't a single mother. Neither our finances nor our principles permitted hired help, so it was again lucky that Kenneth didn't regard fathering as what you do for an hour on Sundays in the backyard with a basketball. Since any child learns more from what is perceived than preached, it was as crucial that Blake saw a man cook, clean, and parent as a matter of course as it was that he saw women act in nontraditional ways.

We started early. When I was pregnant we chose a genderless name for this being whose sex we didn't yet know. Every detail *mattered* to us, passionately; I'm glad, because children *notice* the details. And while I might now wince at certain baby pictures (was it necessary to sew the fisted female symbol on his blanket and teach him the Black Power salute forgodsake?), I can laugh at and forgive most of our excesses; more important, Blake can. It was a frightening time. Vietnam bled across the TV screen each night; friends were going to prison. Activists, we lay awake obsessing over who to name as Blake's guardian if something should happen to us.

We made it up as we went along. Blake—whose permission and advice I sought before writing this piece, since it involved him—helped me remember some of the highs (and lows):

We never lied to him. This was sometimes very hard. When our marriage ended, it was hardest of all. (Friends worried that a child couldn't handle complicated truths, but if you think back to your childhood, it was the complicated *lies* that left scars.) Blake says now that this was one of the best, bravest things we did.

We called each other by our names—never "go to Daddy; see what Mommy thinks"—so we kept our identities as real, fallible people. It helped empower Blake, and made the transition easier on us all as he matured. (When he was about three, Blake experimented with "Mama" and "Daddy" because other kids did it. We said fine, that whatever he'd call us we'd answer. After a week, he shrugged and reverted to our names.)

His earliest bedtime stories had strong female and gentle male characters; we invented them because there were so few antisexist children's books. Some were historical adventures: how the witches were really midwives and healers, how Harriet Tubman smuggled slaves north on the Underground Railroad. Far from "programming" him, we were trying to counter patriarchal programming with family-style affirmative action.

Blake grew up in a home where art was a source of pleasure. He says the message he got when young—that being a creative artist required self-discipline but was still the best fun around—had an even more profound effect than the legacy of politics. (I think they're connected—and confess that though I'd love him even if he were a professional wrestler, I'm awfully relieved he isn't.) Now a composer and songwriter, he plays keyboards and is the lead singer for the band Afterimage.

We talked politics with him, trying, not always successfully, to answer any questions he asked; he never felt mystified about what we were doing or patronized. Soon he was radicalizing *us*, about the power relationship between adults and "short people" (children), about kids' rights, about children's suffrage.

Nothing was proscribed as reading matter or on TV, because we were afraid of the "forbidden fruit" syndrome. (It helped that we were all three avid fans of the "I, Claudius" series, and that Blake and I have been for years not-so-closet Trekkies; we counted it a personal triumph when "where no man has gone before" was changed to "no *one*.") But since we'd all generally discuss what we were reading or had watched, if it seemed that the subject matter demeaned someone's humanity, we'd especially talk about *that*.

The same held true for misbehavior; he was never struck, and rarely punished by losing privileges or being sent to his room. Instead, we'd talk about it—no rhetoric but real-life examples of speech and actions having consequences that could hurt (or heal) people. Blake now loves to tease me about these D & M (Deep and Meaningful) talks. "There were moments," he groans, "when I almost longed to be simply forbidden something or punished, like other kids. But *noooo*. We'd Talk About It." So we overdid it, okay? Given the alternatives, I'd do it again. And I've smiled to myself over the years, overhearing Blake lobby his peers in the same way.

We presented alternatives to patriarchal "norms." He was offered—and played with—dolls as well as fire trucks. True, war toys were not welcome in the house, but when he began eyeing them at other kids' homes, we tried to devise a substitute: medieval legend—Arthur, Guinevere, the Round Table. If he played battle at least it would be with archaic weapons distanced from the reality of Vietnam, so he might be less accepting of the idea that contemporary weapons are toys and vice versa (yes, we Talked About It). I still consider this compromise a fudge. Nevertheless, Blake is strongly antiwar, so something must have worked.

We tried to celebrate, not just promulgate, feminism. Blake recalls the Susan B. Anthony birthday party when he turned ten. Since his birthday falls in July when school was out and his friends were gone, he "shared" a party with S.B.A. on February 15 (the presents were for him, though). Charades were played from hints based on her life; pin-the-tail-on-the-donkey became pin-the-ERA-star-on-the-state with a large map of the U.S.A.; and kids scrambled around a huge homemade crossword puzzle on the floor, collaborating to solve such clues as "Susan B. Anthony fought for the right of women to...." It was a great hit, because making the party educative ran second to making it fun.

Interestingly, what Blake remembers most keenly from his childhood are shared moments of spontaneous jubilation at just being alive: finger painting in the nude at age five with his father and making a splendid mess with impunity; splashing umbrella-less through a summer downpour at age six with me, drenched and laughing so hard we could barely catch our breath. These are moments that transcend gender. Which is the point.

Still, Blake says wryly that his upbringing at times went "a bit over the top." He notes we might have prepared him better for his classmates' reactions when he denounced Thanksgiving as a holiday insulting to Native Americans, protested classroom Halloween decorations depicting witches as warty-nosed horrors, or proclaimed babies were *not* delivered by storks, which was why women should have the right to choose an abortion. He got roughed up for objecting to anti-lesbian/gay remarks and refusing to join other boys in a ritual *Playboy*-centerfold drool on the school bus. (At the time, I was a still-active brown belt—and I found myself having fantasies of practicing on certain ten-year-old bullies.)

We did *try* to warn him, many times and in many ways, that taking stands could get you in trouble and cost you friends. I remember one time in particular, when he was about eight: he had refused to play cowboys and Indians (actually, he'd said he would play, but only if he could be an Indian and if the Indians could win), and the other kids had laughed at him and run off, so he was yet again left out. Like a sense memory of pain, I remember him coming home crying about it, still not understanding the cruelty of it; I remember holding him tightly, crying myself, while I murmured over and over that no one could fight on every front every minute, that you had to be selective, and that he must remember always that our approval and love were never contingent on his carrying these banners. But yes, I know that we also sent a second message, of such pride at his courage (there were lively visits to the principal's office in his defense) that he felt challenged to persist. If I were to do it over, I'd intensify the warnings—but probably be just as unable to contain the pride.

Did we have major doubts? I honestly have to say, "Not really." We truly trusted the politics and tried to live them—and we trusted Blake. We also began to realize that in the long run, it doesn't come down to "divesting" of power, privilege, or anything; it's not a loss, a negative. Rather it's a positive, an addition of consciousness, a building of that old-fashioned thing called character.

Now Blake is a grown man. Happily, he doesn't parrot what I stand for; he's made his politics *his*, by putting his own spin on values he's been raised with. What if rejection of parental values *isn't* a universal process but a symptom of patriarchy? In cultures where a child is parented by the whole tribe, adolescent rebellion doesn't exist—neither does an Oedipal phase.

Part of me is vigilant; the patriarchy is insidious—and it's also dangerous to be smug about one's own man (including a son) being "an exception." No one is. But I *am* proud of what Kenneth and I, together and separately, gave Blake—and of what Blake brought to the equation. I admit to feeling deeply flattered when, for example, he chose to live near me, or wrote an unsentimental but stunning song called "Sunrise" about an early morning beach walk we'd taken together when he was seven—the peach and silver miracle of his very first dawn. So we hold fast—while learning to let go.

Ultimately, it all comes down to love. Not the sugary kind; love fierce and creative enough to demand change—for ourselves, our children, and the planet. *That's* the "mother love" I aspire to.

And they've called me a man-hater for it.

Ask my son if I am.

"Until men are ready to share the responsibilities of full-time, universal child-care as a social priority, their sons and ours will be without any coherent vision of what nonpatriarchal manhood might be."

—Adrienne Rich, *Of Woman Born*

Sean Mancuso Longdon, age 8.

Sean with mother Carolina Mancuso.

"But Will He Be a 'Normal' Boy?"
–Raising a Feminist Son

Carolina Mancuso

In the photo he's wearing a plaid shirt with the sleeves rolled up. The end of his belt dangles from the loop of his jeans and he's wearing the watch his classmates gave him as a going-away present, along with a guinea pig. Instead of the usual kitchen paraphernalia, there are boxes, a pail, crinkled newspapers scattered about in the background, no counters, and no curtains on the one window off to the side and across the very tiny room. Just out of range is the variety of cleaners and rags and hammers and screwdrivers strewn about from the day's cleaning and unpacking. Directly behind him is the stove which is still too dirty to use.

That, in fact, is why Sean stands at the only table, which happens to be the perfect height for a smallish eight-year-old and has enough surface to hold the electric fry pan, a bowl and not much else. He's wielding a wooden spoon, about to turn a piece of chicken as the picture is snapped unexpectedly and from the side so there's no awareness of the moment being caught, just total involvement in the task.

When he was five years old and we'd already been a single-parent family for a year, I told him it was time to learn to cook and that at least one supper a week would be his responsibility. The early stuff—toast and eggs, macaroni and cheese—soon gave way to natural interests and inclinations to experiment so that by eight, he had a fairly wide repertoire of standard menus and was beginning to compose recipes of his own. By 12, he could handle complicated French cuisine but when he returned home from college with his own adaptation of my Italian mother's precious recipe for tomato sauce, I registered my shock, swallowed my indignation, and had to admit it was—not hers but—pretty damned good. Since then, after our many years of near-vegetarianism, he has moved beyond me into veganism and—I guess you'd call it— vegan gourmet. To the delight of his *compañera*, in their household he's been primary cook.

This young man, I said to myself, will not relegate cooking to a woman.

People might say, well, so he had a natural inclination, and true enough it might be. But there was no way that cooking was going to be the only survival skill he developed. Despite my family's shock at my lifestyle—this was the early 1970s, in a place and a time that preceded the acceptance of divorce, single-parenting, working mothers, the acknowledgment of day care as a viable option and even the pretense of equal-pay-for-equal-work—I was determined to change the parenting patterns that hadn't worked on me as a child, repeat the ones that had, and do it all with a feminist consciousness. Determined, that is, to raise a feminist-thinking son.

In our single-mother household, money was always a problem. I did part-time and freelance work so I could be around as much as possible for his growing-up time, and compensated the low income by sharing living space and household expenses with others whenever possible. Such an arrangement meant that there were other people around—people to interact with, to have to consider, to learn to live with. When it was a house shared with other mothers and kids, it also meant that he, an only child, had to adjust to something like a sibling relationship. Neither the arrangements nor the housemates were always easy nor were they ones that Sean would have picked, and he did a fair amount of complaining about our housing situations, although there were periods when he really enjoyed them. We managed housework by hanging up a chart on the wall with everybody taking a particular job for a period of time. Sean's was one of the names on that chart, so his responsibilities around the house were clearly stated. And he was clearly expected, like everyone else, me included, to carry them out.

This young man, I said to myself, will not depend on a woman to clean for him.

But those were the easy things, the things you could be teaching to raise an independent son, not necessarily one with a raised consciousness about the role of women in the world. That was the harder part— to make an unpopular subject in the culture-at-large a common reference point at home. I did it by talking (probably at times too much), by having conversations on the way things were around us and in the news. By analyzing situations. By sharing what I knew of history. By letting him know about some of the obstacles I myself faced. By listening to him, to his observations and feelings and thoughts.

That communication between us came from an already long history of openness and respect. I believe that children learn to listen by being listened to, learn politeness by having it practiced on them, learn respect—a right not only of adults but also of children—by having respectfulness directed towards them. I had learned these attitudes toward children from my father who deeply influenced my conscious choices as a parent. But I remembered well the grown-ups who had not treated me with respect, who had either put me down or patronized me. And I recalled children who had already learned to treat their peers that way. I was not going to repeat the pattern. I saw how commonplace it was, how matter-of-factly it was already being exercised on my child: the many times, for instance, that people who stopped to talk to him when he was a baby or toddler in a stroller would start or end up by saying something about his thumb being in his mouth, the kind of comment those people wouldn't think of making to an adult. As time went on, I talked such situations over with him, gave him my view, my recognition of his hurt or embarrassment or anger.

This young man, I said to myself, will not be insensitive to other people's feelings, nor to his own.

When he was a toddler and his father was still with us, we lived in an apartment complex just outside of the small city where I grew up. The complex was an enclave of young couples and small children, where the mothers occasionally coffee-klatsched while the kids played. I soon had gained a reputation for weirdness by being the only one who would not hit her child. I had never been hit and could only wonder why people imagined physical violence could build a sense of responsibility and good behavior. When the inevitable tussles among the preschoolers erupted at our little gatherings, and one mother after another jumped up to smack her kid, I would pull Sean aside and discuss what was and was not acceptable behavior. Sometimes that talk was harsh. I didn't hold back the anger that was a consequence of his actions. Nor did I refrain from removing him from the situation, insisting he sit out some of the playtime, or sending him alone to his room when we were at home. But I couldn't see how the screams provoked by slapping and spanking inspired change or motivated good behavior. It just indicated that might could pretend that it was right.

This young man, I said to myself, is not going to be trained, however subtly, in violence.

It wasn't just the no-spanking that made us an anomaly which the other mothers—neighbors and friends—couldn't understand and therefore teased us about. They were also highly amused by the fact that Sean had no guns to play with, no G.I. Joe, no toys of violence. Even my family was worried about that one. They might understand and even be amused by the cooking and the cleaning, but could he possibly grow up "normal" without "boy" toys to play with? The real day of reckoning arrived when I gave Sean a doll—a baby doll, and a Black baby doll at that—at a holiday gathering with my family.

This young man, I said to myself, must be prepared for parenting.

Family and community attitudes weren't the only obstacles. There were innumerable others, large and small, all along the way. When he was still very young well-meaning relatives fed him candy and cookies against my will. I learned I could not keep television away from him, though we didn't own one for quite a while and when we did the viewing was limited. I learned eventually to relax and to believe that my pointing out the "playful" violence in Disney cartoons and the sexism in Popeye would make a difference in how and what he saw. I learned to believe also in the eventual if not immediate benefit of reviewing even our favorite children's books for sexism in illustration or text. I learned that I always had to explain why I was compelled to swim upstream not just to Sean but to everyone around. And of course, I couldn't resist explaining even to some who didn't ask. It came with the territory: these alternative choices were not just a passing fancy; I had made them consciously and with deep conviction. And didn't I want other children to grow up the same way? I was ready, if not always energized, to tell people why I chose to do things as I did. But such explanations are better made without being defensive—and I never could get used to the lack of openness I frequently encountered. Lucky for me, some of the women from the consciousness-raising group that had helped to change my thinking still lived nearby. And luckily for Sean and me, some of the time we lived in a tiny but thriving alternative community of people.

Like any effort to raise consciousness, trying to be a feminist parent—to translate feminist understanding into the role of parent—requires an enormous commitment to self-reflection and self-change. It requires a willingness to reject the old ways of doing things and to accept improvising the new ways. Like many other women, I kept a journal which helped me understand the world around me and examine my own life and language and behavior. In our society, there is little or no focused education on parenting. We are all pretty much on our own in the quest for role models, beliefs and values which will help us break new ground.

But, although I call these characteristics of "feminist" parenting, should-n't critical thinking, for example—be part of *all* parenting, after all?

This young man, I said to myself, must not be afraid to think critically, to reflect on his own life and, when necessary, to stand apart from the crowd.

In the fourth grade at a new school the year after we moved to New York City—not long after that photo in the kitchen was taken—Sean took to reading Tin-Tin comic books in school when he was bored. His teacher thought the act required discipline (rather than understanding the motivation) so he said that when the class walked to the playground and back, Sean would have to walk at the end of the girls' line.

That there were separate lines for boys and for girls was enough to set me off. But the thought that a boy would be taught to consider being with girls as shame and humiliation....I marched to school, sat down at Mr. H's desk, and patiently (though somewhat hotly, I'm sure) explained my thinking. To his credit, he was willing to listen, and to apologize, admitting he had never thought of it that way. And years later, he still remembered and greeted me warmly on the street.

This young man, I said to myself, must think of women as people to be respected.

One of his first male friends in that school was a boy whose parents also packed his lunch with whole wheat bread and yogurt. Sean and Jeremy found each other quickly, and a friendship grew between them and the two families that thrives to this day. Over the years I've watched Sean and Jeremy as consciously feminist young men confront all kinds of attitudes towards women and the men who befriend them. They con-tinually live against the grain, searching out others (unfortunately not a majority) who also were raised or came to consciousness like them. It was a great relief that their friends in high school and college did more group socializing than dating and pairing off. But even among them the underlying attitudes towards women did not reflect real change. I felt a deep commitment to providing the kind of home where he would feel free to bring his friends, where they could have privacy and a sense of ease, and where their conversations alone and with adults could flow freely on any topic. Most important was the sense that we were all engaged in a process of growth, teenager and adult, searching for answers, uncovering even more questions.

Finding men to be role models was a continual struggle. Some of my male friends were trying to live by the hard-won changes they had made, and I was grateful for that. It was not until Sean was 15 that I made a

179

long-lasting commitment with a man who could truly be called a feminist. It's been a shared venture since then.

This young man, I said to myself, must see men as gentle as well as strong and must not be threatened by women who are equally strong and gentle.

At its most basic, I think feminist parenting is about collaboration, about examining the power structure of relationships between people, between women and men, especially as manifested in the family where it all begins. It's about being willing to alter that power structure, to make it more democratic, but not by abandoning the guidance of adult experience. Rather, it's about searching for the balance: valuing new and youthful perspectives while maintaining authority when and where needed. It's about working together, about seeing ourselves, young and old, as agents for a changing world.

This young man, I said to myself, must learn to collaborate rather than compete.

Well, all this sounds a bit idyllic, doesn't it? Easy? Smooth? Ha!

There were the usual parenting issues: contradictions, inconsistencies, dilemmas, challenges, confusion, apparent failures, and strayings from the track. And these issues were complicated by our perspective on the culture around us. And then there were the plain old tough spots. The day Sean bit his two-year-old best friend so hard we had to rush her to the hospital. The day I suddenly understood what drives people to physical abuse, and locked him in his room so I could get my anger in hand. The Christmas season when we argued constantly about the worth of owning an action figure of Six Million Dollar Man. There were the years of "disequilibrium"—age four which I've always thought was really two-with-a-mouth, eleven when he took to telling my dates how they'd better behave, sixteen when he left Model Congress to have a real "businessman's lunch," sparking a call to me from the principal.

You can plant the seeds, but you really can't predict the outcome. You can do only what you think best and you have to keep on believing in the process. I felt all along that Sean was working with me, that we were growing together. I could see the shadow of the man he was growing to be slowly come into focus—kind, sensitive, gentle, patient, interested in people and in how they treat each other. I heard how other people responded to him and he to them. And when in his early 20s, his *compañera* thanked me for raising him the way I did, I breathed a sigh of relief.

"What do we want for our sons? Women who have begun to challenge the values of patriarchy are haunted by this question. We want them to remain, in the deepest sense, sons of the mother, yet also to grow into themselves, to discover new ways of being men even as we are discovering new ways of being women."

—Adrienne Rich, *Of Woman Born*

Claire Braz-Valentine and sons.

For Every Mother Everywhere

Claire Braz-Valentine

My sons, I love you.
But I have just discovered that if I take your ages and add them up,
I've been mothering for almost twice as long as I've been living.
I have been mothering through six years of real cloth diapers,
and two years of projectile vomiting and three years of orange juice
    allergies.
I have purchased two hundred and thirty seven pairs of tennis shoes,
and patched over twenty yards of materials onto various pairs of jeans,
and I have cooked a logging truck of hot dogs.
I have explained wet dreams as if I really understood them.
I have read Winnie The Pooh until I began to sound like Eeyore.
You have written on my walls with lipstick.
You have broken my heirloom plates,
and a million glasses,
and every watch you ever had,
a hundred watches,
all accidents.
You have lost every sweater,
and a mountain of caps,
and even your shoes one day in the street
right before the street sweeper truck came and swept them away,
and you've lost enough socks to swathe the world in warmth for the winter.
You have dressed my dog in your clothing.
You have eaten her dog food.
You have eaten dirt,
and a house full of cookies,
and no squash.
You have made me fourteen pencil cups from orange juice cans,
wrapped carefully around and around with colored yarn,
and then lost all my pencils.
You have forgotten every telephone message,
every note from your teachers,
every bedtime,

and where you put anything always.
You have collected the world in little scraps on your bedroom shelves,
shelves full of plastic monsters,
glow in the dark Frankensteins,
laughing Draculas,
leering werewolves,
all watching peacefully over you through the night.
You have slept with teddy bears, and dogs and dolls, and cats,
and pieces of your erector set, Lincoln Logs, and Tinker Toys.
You have become agnostic pacifists.
You have become the new feminist males.
You have been called gifted,
and yet you have cried over the Monopoly game when I took your property.
And I wanted to tell you, that sometimes when I talk about you
and all you have done,
and all you are planning to do,
I sometimes think
I should have had girls instead.
I should have saved my money instead.
I should have traveled.
And I just wanted to tell you,
I'm glad I didn't.

"But, having borne three sons, I found myself living, at the deepest levels of passion and confusion, with three small bodies, soon three persons, whose care I often felt was eating away at my life, but whose beauty, humor, and physical affection were amazing to me. I saw them, not as 'sons' and potential inheritors of patriarchy, but as the sweet flesh of infants, the delicate insistency of exploring bodies, the purity of concentration, grief, or joy which exists undiluted in young children..."

—Adrienne Rich, *Of Woman Born*

Barbara Miller and sons.

An Equitable Plan

Barbara Miller

While I was pregnant with my first child I read several bits of advice on parenting which I held close, awaiting the time I would need them. The first, related to equitable sharing, was, "Have one child divide the amount of the treat in half; the other gets first pick." The second could be titled, "How to arrive home to a peaceful atmosphere." The advice was, "When the kids are old enough to stay home alone, put everyone in charge, by paying them each an equal amount upon your return if the kitchen is clean and there are no reports of fights." I have been able to use both these items to great advantage over the course of my seventeen years of mothering; however, it was the third bit of advice, aimed at making every day "Mother's Day," that I saved for the big time.

My oldest son was three when I gave birth to twin boys, and they were seven and four years old when their dad and I separated. They have grown up between two homes, with parents who respect one another and parent in a similar and communicative manner. They have seen their dad cook, sew, and do laundry, and their mom put up window screens, buy cars, and fix bikes. No mystique here about what is "men's" or "women's" work. As the boys have grown older and stronger I have delegated many chores requiring brute strength to them. They have all also done laundry, vacuumed, and cleaned the bathroom. I love to nurture and cook for them, and I recall with fondness and appreciation how my mom always had my clothes clean and my lunch packed. I've tried to pass on the favors to my sons. However, this past spring I found myself working overtime as a wage earner, and coming home to domestic responsibilities with little appreciation or assistance from my sons. I waited for the right moment, and then I sprung my last, long-stored piece of parenting advice upon them.

It went like this. At dinner one night I lamented on the lack of help I was receiving. One of the twins piped up with the comment, "You don't do anything anyhow." His older brother agreed, and that was my cue. "You're on," I said. "From now on I do nothing."

Now, dear reader, I do not need to list all the things I really do (shopping, transportation, food dispersal, etc.), but at that moment I saw a

187

vision of my true release from bondage. I would live up to their expectations and I WOULD DO NOTHING!!! I could hardly wait to begin!

This delightful dinner conversation occurred on a Friday night. The next morning the boys left for their dad's for the weekend. I cleaned up enough to assuage my need for order, and then worked on my plan.

In my culture, food equates with love. To give up that aspect of mothering would be difficult. Now, there was, and always is, enough food in our house to feed a starving family of four for at least a month. The boys might not like canned beans and soup, but they certainly would not go hungry. However, anyone who has ever fed and housed teenage boys knows there is one item, which when absent, will bring them to their knees: milk. I knew they could not exist 20 minutes without milk, yet I was determined not to go to the store because "I do nothing." After debating the options with several other moms (Do I pull out the emergency supply of powdered milk? Provide milk but no other basics? Do nothing and see what happens?), I came up with the following compromise. I would provide money for the purchase of milk, but not the use of my car. They would be free to ride their bikes the 10 minute jaunt to the store and lug the milk back.

There. I had fulfilled my motherly needs and duties, but they would be ultimately responsible.

Monday afternoon I arrived home from work about 4:30 p.m. and my eldest asked, "What's for dinner?" I replied, "I wouldn't know," reminded him that "I do nothing" and outlined specifically what "nothing" entailed. No meals, no grocery shopping, no transportation, no laundry, and most importantly, *no milk delivery*! I then left for a walk.

The fine art of negotiation is one thing I hope my children learn from living with one another. Although they vastly prefer brute force, I continually and consistently stress that they have to talk out problems and compromise. This, along with teaching them to hang up their towels, is a gift I would like to give to my future daughters-in-law. Throughout the years their success rate in negotiation has been climbing, and at times I fear that I have actually raised three budding defense attorneys! Still, I was always surprised whenever their negotiations actually worked, when a compromise was reached without the threat of bloodshed. So, when they asked, as I jauntily left for my evening exercise, what it would take to get me OFF strike, I replied, "Come up with a plan where the three of you share in some of the household chores and responsibilities, then prove to me you will follow through." With that, I took off with a smile on my face, lightness in my step, and delight in that I didn't have to cook dinner, clean up, or do laundry. This, I thought, I could get used to!

While I was gone (and this was a long walk, including a lengthy visit at a friend's house) I found myself hoping that this strike could go on and on.

Three hours later I returned home. As I walked in I found all three boys huddled around the kitchen table formulating lists of chores and the assignments of such. They pleaded with me to be seated and hear their plan.

They had listed all the things mom really *does* do, and seemingly without physical violence had parceled them out to each other. They had divided the chores into levels of difficulty, responsibility and frequency so that no one felt overburdened. The formulation of this plan was amazing; coming through in performance would be a miracle. We worked out a few of the fine details, for instance, what if the trash is overflowing, and it isn't your job, but your brother isn't home? (Answer: someone else has to do it.) And what if they start the laundry, but then need to get to bed. If I am still up, would I please put it in the dryer? (I'm not *totally* unreasonable.) I relented for the night—they could have the car to go buy milk, since they had come up with such an equitable plan. However, I was still officially on strike until I saw that the plan was actually in effect.

It is now three months later. For the most part, the boys have carried out their part of the deal. I admit to doing most of the family meal preparation, but I rarely whip up individual snacks for them. One of the twins lucked out with his chore list—many of his duties became almost obsolete. (The cat litter rarely needed to be changed once spring weather arrived.) There is some renegotiation and fine tuning to be done for summertime, and if everyone is willing to add yard chores and deep housecleaning, there could be a weekly allowance in store. Best of all, one of them got mad at me and refused to help me with an unassigned task. "Why should I?" he asked. "You don't do anything for me." I responded immediately with, "You're on—I'll do nothing for you," and an apology was quickly forthcoming.

Will this work? Will there be long-term effects? I think so.

Brian Voss, Larry Voss, and Carol Gill.

Shattering Two Molds:
Feminist Parents with Disabilities

Carol J. Gill and Larry A. Voss

We are two persons with extensive physical disabilities who have raised a nondisabled son. Countering the stereotype of people with disabilities as childlike, fragile, and suffering, we have nurtured and, we believe, nurtured powerfully. With wonder and relief, we have watched our child's development into a generous, emotionally open, strong, and socially responsible adult. It was not a snap. All three of us waged a long struggle against society's devaluation of human difference to get to this place.

Our war against ableist beliefs began in childhood when we acquired our disabilities in the 1950 polio epidemic. We used braces and wheelchairs and would have had little problem attending our neighborhood school if not for architecture and its real foundation: attitudes. In those days before the disability rights movement, we were barred from mainstream life. No ramps or elevators were installed to ensure our access. Instead, we were bussed miles each day to a "special" school with similarly displaced children.

Undoubtedly, these experiences laid the groundwork for our acceptance of a feminist perspective. We acquired a deep suspicion of unequal treatment and stereotyping in any form. In high school, we identified with the civil rights struggle. In college, our rejection of sexism took definite shape. For Carol, the conscious decision to participate in the women's movement grew from classroom discussion of the work of Greer, Friedan, and Steinem. For Larry, it grew out of heated ideological debates between men and women in radical student collectives during the antiwar movement.

When Larry married a woman from this movement (his first marriage), he found daily life to be a mixture of new and traditional gender roles. During most of the marriage, his partner, who was not disabled, worked as an intensive care nurse while Larry completed his education. Although they shared household duties according to preferences as well as Larry's disability limitations, it was expected that his partner would cook and perform "housewife" chores after coming home from her job.

The decision to have a baby, on the other hand, was planned to be as joint a venture as possible. Larry remained by his wife's side during her prenatal exams and, long before it was accepted practice, he participated in the birth of his son in the hospital delivery room. He remembers this experience as ecstasy and agony—the incomparable joy of watching his child's birth and his sense of helpless horror as the emerging head made an audible tear in his wife's tissues. That painful moment registered clearly in Larry's consciousness—a factor, perhaps, in his later diligence in shouldering childcare duties.

Larry, in fact, became the primary parent. As is true of most children of disabled parents, Brian had little trouble adapting to his father's wheelchair and unconventional strategies for accomplishing daily tasks. When Larry's marriage foundered, he had no intention of parting with his son, then a toddler. Although it was rare for men to get custody of children in divorces, and even rarer for disabled persons, Larry fought to keep Brian with him and won.

Single parenthood was a rich and difficult time for them. Although Larry's sister and mother helped baby-sit, he experienced the loneliness and weight of responsibility that many single parents face. Additionally, there were unique physical and social difficulties. Unemployed and without child support, Larry could afford neither personal assistance nor adequate accessible housing. Consequently, errands such as grocery shopping became all-day feats of endurance. After driving home from the store, he would be forced to leave his wheelchair at the top of the stairs, crawl down the steps several times to his basement apartment and up again, hauling each bag of groceries followed by the baby, and then drag his wheelchair down the steps so he could get back into it and put groceries away!

Even more exhausting were the social hurdles. Strangers as well as family members challenged Larry's decision to keep his child, citing both gender- and disability-based concerns. Brian's first teachers suggested he was being shortchanged by not having a mother or nondisabled parent. (Brian's biological mother moved out of state and maintained very limited contact with him.) Neighborhood children teased or grilled him about his "wheelchair father" and asked why he had no mother. People who knew nothing about Larry's parenting skills would cluck over Brian's misfortune and tell him that having a "crippled daddy" was his cross to bear.

192

Although we—Carol and Larry—knew each other superficially while attending the same "special" high school, our paths did not cross again until a mutual friend brought us together at the time of Larry's divorce. After several years of intense and romantic friendship, we married.

At first, Brian was thrilled about Carol joining the family. Even before the wedding, which took place when he was seven, he insisted on calling her "Mom." But once it was official, he was ambivalent. Due both to her disability and her feminism, Brian's "new mother" was anything but the traditional nurturing figure people had told him he needed. She was physically incapable of performing many of the cooking and household chores mothers were supposed to do. She was not conventionally pretty. She was unexpectedly strong in communicating her ideas and affecting household decisions. She was even unwilling to change her name when she got married.

Not that Brian had been raised to be sexist. He had a father who baked cookies, cared for a home, brushed his lover's hair, and became an elementary school teacher. He also knew Larry's fondness for baseball, tools, and macho action movies. Father and son openly shared hugs and kisses between bouts of arm wrestling. Larry's philosophy of child-rearing, like his philosophy of education, stressed openness. He had always been pleased that Brian's early years were fairly non-sex typed. He had let the toddler's strawberry blond hair grow to shoulder length undaunted by family predictions of gender confusion. He admired Brian's eclectic taste in toy trucks and stuffed animals as well as his drawings of kittens, nudes, Army tanks, Spiderman and posies.

But despite Larry's efforts to raise a child liberated from all the "isms," Brian was exposed to and affected by the sexism and ableism (not to mention racism, ethnocentrism, and heterosexism) of the surrounding culture. Dealing with this in addition to the typical tensions of stepparenting introduced a great deal of struggle into our family life.

It is hard for us to separate where our parenting was guided by feminism or by our experience and values as disabled persons. We believe in both notions of a women's culture and a disabled people's culture. Further, we believe the overlap of cultural values in the two communities is significant. Both feminist analysis and the disability independent living philosophy embrace values of interdependence, cooperative problem-solving, flexibility/adaptability, and the importance of relationships in contrast to traditional male values of autonomy, performance, competition, dominance, and acquisition.

By necessity, a guiding principle of our partnership has always been unfettered cooperation. There has been no "women's work" or "men's work." From the start, we negotiated most tasks of life by deciding who could do it, who was good at it, who wanted to do it, who had time, who needed help, etc. Larry's arm strength meant he had kitchen duty. Carol's greater physical limitations meant she organized the lists and schedules. In our professional jobs, we alternated being the major breadwinner. Everything from lovemaking to getting out of the car was an exercise in cooperation and respect—an orchestration of timing, assistance, and down-to-earth tolerance.

Our parenting was similarly orchestrated. As the only one who could drive, Larry did the car-pooling. Carol's math acuity made her the homework authority. Larry did more of the "hands-on" parenting jobs: cuddling, restraining, washing, roughhousing. Carol nurtured by story-telling, instructing, reprimanding, discussing, and watching endlessly ("Mom, watch this!").

We both did an enormous amount of talking. Larry explained and lectured. Carol questioned motivations and articulated feelings. We even entered family counseling during several difficult times to talk some more. Reflecting back on it, we realize one of the central themes of all this talking was nurturance: caring for and being responsible for people, animals, plants, and the environment. Larry encouraged empathy in Brian through questions like, "How do you think you would feel if that happened to you?" Carol nudged Brian to write notes and make gifts for family members. We gave him regular chores to do for the family and engaged him in many rescues of abandoned and injured stray animals.

Another major theme was prejudice and unfairness. Disability rights and women's rights were frequent topics in our household. Carol often directed Brian's attention to surrounding events, attitudes, and images that contributed to women's oppression, e.g., *Playboy*, sadistic images in rock videos, crude jokes. Most of the time, Brian would roll his eyes and protest that Carol could find sexism in anything. Larry usually backed her up but sometimes he lightened the tension by joining Brian in teasing Carol about her unwillingness to take her menfolk's last name. This was a family joke that ironically conveyed both affection and respect for Carol and got everyone to smile.

We also did a lot of the standard things most people do to raise a nonsexist son, from respecting his need to cry, to encouraging his interests and talents regardless of their traditional "gender appropriateness."

Again, this lent a certain eclecticism to Brian's activities which included sports, cooking, ceramics, drawing, music, reading, swimming and surfing, collecting, etc. On both feminist and pacifist grounds, we tried to avoid the most destructive "macho" stuff. For example, at his request, we enrolled Brian in a karate class. But when we discovered the instructor tested each boy's mettle by getting the class to take turns punching him in the stomach, Larry pronounced it barbaric and encouraged Brian to drop out, which he did. We also kept Brian out of formal team sports run by zealous competitive coaches and pressured him not to join the military when the gung-ho recruiters tried to nab him in high school.

Although we often held little hope that our battle against the "isms" was making an impact, like other parents, we now see that children do pay attention. Brian is now 22 and spontaneously uses words like "sexism" when critiquing the world. He is also our only relative who consistently uses Carol's proper name in introductions and addressing mail. He is comfortable in the friendship of both men and women. He loves sports and still hugs his childhood stuffed dog when he's sick. He has argued for the rights of women, people with disabilities, and other minorities.

Brian has shared his life for four years with a woman who also has strong goals and opinions. They have found a way to support each other, argue, and give space as needed. Like us, they are lover, companion, and family—equals. Seeing them interact is the great payoff to all our years of struggle. We enjoy watching our son laundering his partner's delicate sweaters or lovingly constructing her sandwiches. We listen to him express the depth of his feelings and respect for her. (Yes, he is a talker like his parents!) They have negotiated their course with cooperation, nurturance, and concern about unfairness. They want to have a family; they want to protect the earth.

When we told Brian about writing this piece, we asked his permission to tell the story of our family. He was enthusiastic and helped us reminisce about the past. One of his recollections confirmed how much he had been affected by the equity in his parents' relationship. He told us that sometimes as a child when he would answer the family telephone, callers would ask to speak to the "head of the house." Brian remembers his natural response to this request was to ask "Which one?" Then he and the caller would have a confusing discussion about which parent was needed on the phone. He said it was always simpler when only one of us was home because then the choice was clear: he would just summon whichever "head of the house" happened to be present!

Challenges (an excerpt)

Jean Ellis

I failed to think through how, bringing up Daniel on my own, I would confront issues to do with gender and race, although I recognized that these issues would be important. In fact, in order to bring up a boy to be gentle and caring and in touch with his feelings, I felt his father's absence was almost essential, given his own stereotypical views of what constituted acceptable male behavior. But on issues of race identity and racism, I had to regret that we were not together. Pierre-Marie is so strong and secure in his identity as an African. I would have liked Daniel to have been closer to that.

The assumptions in Cameroonian society about a woman's role in the family, and my own experience in relation to men while there, were undoubtedly the reasons why I could not live in Cameroon on a permanent basis. The basic attitudes in Britain and Cameroon are not so very different, but in Britain it is easier, at least at the personal level, to escape them to a degree. My feelings were reconfirmed by my first visit back to Cameroon when Daniel was a baby. On my only holiday since my pregnancy, I not only spent the entire time traipsing to the market and staggering back with food and bottles of beer for Pierre-Marie's friends to drink to Daniel's health, cooking and cleaning in the heat without the benefit of appliances but, even more infuriating, I was not allowed to discuss such things as financial matters. (As if I had not managed my life entirely alone for the last year.) Even Daniel, a 9-month-old baby, was not allowed in the kitchen; it was no place for a boy, his father said.

Raising Daniel alone, I was able to bring up a son who was aware of gender inequalities and who valued women and girls in a way which remains unusual among young boys. One of Daniel's earliest toys which accompanied him everywhere was a small doll. I banned weapons. I even took out the tiny bullets which came with spaceships and rendered them useless as fighting machines. Without guns, Daniel never rushed around play shooting, and I always felt somewhat impatient with parents who claimed that even if they did not give their boys guns, they would use a stick or their fingers to "shoot" with. This simply did not happen to us. And Daniel never got into fights as often as his friends did.

196

I was also highly selective about programs watched on television. There were never arguments; we simply did something else.

Daniel had a gentle nature from an early age, but I am sure it would have been easy not to have encouraged it, to have persuaded him into more acceptable male behavior or pursuits. Although I think books, television, and toys present messages to children, there are other, more important influences, such as the time spent playing with children far younger than he. Moreover, his music and dancing have also been important, bringing him frequently into the company of girls, away from the endless round of football or skateboarding.

I never had any doubts about any of these things and feel enormously proud of the person Daniel has become. Yet, as he has grown older, I have probably compromised more. He retreats into silence at times, behavior I have found so difficult to accept in adult men. I hope I will come to terms with it, and whatever else emerges as he takes an ever-increasing role in shaping his own character. It will be a struggle for me, I am sure of that. I have accepted that there will be a compromise between my ideals and the reality presented by society as it is now, but I also wonder if I simply do not see the issues as clearly as I did when Daniel was younger. As I turn back to finding my own creativity and a new personal direction, perhaps I simply do not care as much.

As for my bringing Daniel up as a black child, there are two strands to this issue. One is his need to relate to his Cameroonian family and culture as well as to his white family. The second concerns being black in a multiracial society still dominated by white values and power structure. The essential fact is that my black son lives with a white mother while his black father lives thousands of miles away. My most important task has been to give Daniel an enormous amount of self-esteem and confidence, and I think I have done that. Perhaps too well, some might say, but I believe that he will need it on the day that racism properly knocks on his door.

Indeed, we have already encountered a full range of reactions to us as a family unit. At one end of the spectrum there is overt revulsion. One stranger approached me in the park and said, "I can see that you love your baby, but how could you have done such a thing?" I have no answers for such people, not even anger. Because we feel so totally right together, it never occurs to me to ask others for their views. At a personal level, their hang-ups are simply not my concern. Less extreme, there is no doubt that people make assumptions about us. Some people have assumed that Daniel is adopted or that the relationship between

Daniel's father and me did not work or could not work, in no way the whole truth. Pierre-Marie has visited London three times now, and this year Daniel is planning to visit Cameroon on his own for the first time. It has worked exactly as we planned. Pierre-Marie and I are still loving friends, and do meet crazily and romantically at airports every few years. So perhaps for these reasons I feel a particular happiness when we are all together—as if that is a more complete statement.

Man Child: A Black Lesbian Feminist's Response
(an excerpt)

Audre Lorde

I have two children: a fifteen-and-a-half-year-old daughter Beth, and a fourteen-year-old son Jonathan. This is the way it was/is with me and Jonathan, and I leave the theory to another time and person. This is one woman's telling.

I have no golden message about the raising of sons for other lesbian mothers, no secret to transpose your questions into certain light. I have my own ways of rewording those same questions, hoping we will all come to speak those questions and pieces of our lives we need to share. We are women making contact within ourselves and with each other across the restrictions of a printed page, bent upon the use of our own/one another's knowledges.

The truest direction comes from inside. I give the most strength to my children by being willing to look within myself, and by being honest with them about what I find there, without expecting a response beyond their years. In this way they begin to learn to look beyond their own fears.

All our children are outriders for a queendom not yet assured.

My adolescent son's growing sexuality is a conscious dynamic between Jonathan and me. It would be presumptuous of me to discuss Jonathan's sexuality here, except to state my belief that whomever he chooses to explore this area with, his choices will be nonoppressive, joyful, and deeply felt from within, places of growth.

One of the difficulties in writing this piece has been temporal; this is the summer when Jonathan is becoming a man, physically. And our sons must become men—such men as we hope our daughters, born and unborn, will be pleased to live among. Our sons will not grow into women. Their way is more difficult than that of our daughters, for they must move away from us, without us. Hopefully, our sons have what they have learned from us, and a howness to forge it into their own image.

Our daughters have us, for measure or rebellion or outline or dream; but the sons of lesbians have to make their own definitions of self as men. This is both power and vulnerability. The sons of lesbians have the advantage of our blueprints for survival, but they must take what we know and transpose it into their own maleness. May the goddess be kind to my son, Jonathan.

Recently I have met young Black men about whom I am pleased to say that their future and their visions, as well as their concerns within the present, intersect more closely with Jonathan's than do my own. I have shared vision with these men as well as temporal strategies for our survivals and I appreciate the spaces in which we could sit down together. Some of these men I met at the First Annual Conference of Third World Lesbians and Gays held in Washington, D.C., in October, 1979. I have met others in different places and do not know how they identify themselves sexually. Some of these men are raising families alone. Some have adopted sons. They are Black men who dream and who act and who own their feelings, questioning. It is heartening to know our sons do not step out alone.

When Jonathan makes me angriest, I always say he is bringing out the testosterone in me. What I mean is that he is representing some piece of myself as a woman that I am reluctant to acknowledge or explore. For instance, what does "acting like a man" mean? For me, what I reject? For Jonathan, what he is trying to redefine?

Raising Black children—female and male—in the mouth of a racist, sexist, suicidal dragon is perilous and chancy. If they cannot love and resist at the same time, they will probably not survive. And in order to survive they must let go. This is what mothers teach—love, survival—that is, self-definition and letting go. For each of these, the ability to feel strongly and to recognize those feelings is central: how to feel love, how to neither discount fear nor be overwhelmed by it, how to enjoy feeling deeply.

I wish to raise a Black man who will not be destroyed by, nor settle for, those corruptions called *power* by the white fathers who mean his destruction as surely as they mean mine. I wish to raise a Black man who will recognize that the legitimate objects of his hostility are not women, but the particulars of a structure that programs him to fear and despise women as well as his own Black self.

For me, this task begins with teaching my son that I do not exist to do his feeling for him.

Men who are afraid to feel must keep women around to do their feeling for them while dismissing us for the same supposedly "inferior" capacity to feel deeply. But in this way also, men deny themselves their own essential humanity, becoming trapped in dependency and fear.

As a Black woman committed to a liveable future, and as a mother loving and raising a boy who will become a man, I must examine all my possibilities of being within such a destructive system.

Jonathan was three-and-one-half when Frances, my lover, and I met; he was seven when we all began to live together permanently. From the start, Frances' and my insistence that there be no secrets in our household about the fact that we were lesbians has been the source of problems and strengths for both children. In the beginning, this insistence grew out of the knowledge, on both our parts, that whatever was hidden out of fear could always be used either against the children or ourselves—one imperfect but useful argument for honesty. The knowledge of fear can help make us free.

For survival, Black children in america must be raised to be warriors. For survival, they must also be raised to recognize the enemy's many faces. Black children of lesbian couples have an advantage because they learn, very early, that oppression comes in many different forms, none of which have anything to do with their own worth.

To help give me perspective, I remember that for years, in the name-calling at school, boys shouted at Jonathan not—"your mother's a lesbian"—but rather—"your mother's a nigger."

When Jonathan was eight years old and in the third grade we moved, and he went to a new school where his life was hellish as a new boy on the block. He did not like to play rough games. He did not like to fight. He did not like to stone dogs. And all this marked him early on as an easy target.

When he came in crying one afternoon, I heard from Beth how the corner bullies were making Jonathan wipe their shoes on the way home whenever Beth wasn't there to fight them off. And when I heard that the ringleader was a little boy in Jonathan's class his own size, an interesting and very disturbing thing happened to me.

My fury at my own long-ago impotence, and my present pain at his suffering, made me start to forget all that I knew about violence and fear, and blaming the victim, I started to hiss at the weeping child. "The next time you come in here crying...," and I suddenly caught myself in horror.

This is the way we allow the destruction of our sons to begin—in the name of protection and to ease our own pain. My son get beaten up? I was about to demand that he buy that first lesson in the corruption of power, that might makes right. I could hear myself beginning to perpetuate the age-old distortions about what strength and bravery really are.

And no, Jonathan didn't have to fight if he didn't want to, but somehow he did have to feel better about not fighting. An old horror rolled over me of being the fat kid who ran away, terrified of getting her glasses broken.

About that time a very wise woman said to me, "Have you ever told Jonathan that once you used to be afraid, too?"

The idea seemed far-out to me at the time, but the next time he came in crying and sweaty from having run away again, I could see that he felt shamed at having failed me, or some image he and I had created in his head of mother/woman. This image of woman being able to handle it all was bolstered by the fact that he lived in a household with three strong women, his lesbian parents and his forthright older sister. At home, for Jonathan, power was clearly female.

And because our society teaches us to think in an either/or mode—kill or be killed, dominate or be dominated—this meant that he must either surpass or be lacking. I could see the implications of this line of thought. Consider the two western classic myth/models of mother/son relationships: Jocasta/Oedipus, the son who fucks his mother, and Clytemnestra/Orestes, the son who kills his mother.

It all felt connected to me.

I sat down on the hallway steps and took Jonathan on my lap and wiped his tears. "Did I ever tell you about how I used to be afraid when I was your age?"

I will never forget the look on that little boy's face as I told him the tale of my glasses and my after-school fights. It was a look of relief and total disbelief, all rolled into one.

It is as hard for our children to believe that we are not omnipotent as it is for us to know it, as parents. But that knowledge is necessary as the first step in the reassessment of power as something other than might, age, privilege, or the lack of fear. It is an important step for a boy, whose societal destruction begins when he is forced to believe that he can only be strong if he doesn't feel, or if he wins.

I thought about all this one year later when Beth and Jonathan, ten and nine, were asked by an interviewer how they thought they had been affected by being children of a feminist.

Jonathan said that he didn't think there was too much in feminism for boys, although it certainly was good to be able to cry if he felt like it and not to have to play football if he didn't want to. I think of this sometimes now when I see him practicing for his Brown Belt in Tae Kwon Do.

The strongest lesson I can teach my son is the same lesson I teach my daughter: how to be who he wishes to be for himself. And the best way I can do this is to be who I am and hope that he will learn from this not how to be me, which is not possible, but how to be himself. And this means how to move to that voice from within himself, rather than to those raucous, persuasive, or threatening voices from outside, pressuring him to be what the world wants him to be.

And that is hard enough.

Jonathan is learning to find within himself some of the different faces of courage and strength, whatever he chooses to call them. Two years ago, when Jonathan was twelve and in the seventh grade, one of his friends at school who had been to the house persisted in calling Frances "the maid." When Jonathan corrected him, the boy then referred to her as "the cleaning woman." Finally Jonathan said, simply, "Frances is not the cleaning woman, she's my mother's lover." Interestingly enough, it is the teachers at this school who still have not recovered from his openness.

Frances and I were considering attending a Lesbian/Feminist conference this summer, when we were notified that no boys over ten were allowed. This presented logistic as well as philosophical problems for us, and we sent the following letter:

> Sisters:
> Ten years as an interracial lesbian couple has taught us both the dangers of an oversimplified approach to the nature and solutions of any oppression, as well as the danger inherent in an incomplete vision.
> Our thirteen-year-old son represents as much hope for our future world as does our fifteen-year-old daughter, and we are not willing to abandon him to the killing streets of New York City while we journey west to help form a Lesbian-Feminist vision of the future world in which we can all survive and flourish. I hope we can continue this dialogue in the near future, as I feel it is important to our vision and our survival.

The question of separatism is by no means simple. I am thankful that one of my children is male, since that helps to keep me honest. Every line I write shrieks there are no easy solutions.

I grew up in largely female environments, and I know how crucial that has been to my own development. I feel the want and need often for the society of women, exclusively. I recognize that our own spaces are essential for developing and recharging.

As a Black woman, I find it necessary to withdraw into all-Black groups at times for exactly the same reasons—differences in stages of development and differences in levels of interaction. Frequently, when speaking with men and white women, I am reminded of how difficult and time-consuming it is to have to reinvent the pencil every time you want to send a message.

But this does not mean that my responsibility for my son's education stops at age ten, any more than it does for my daughter's. However, for each of them, that responsibility does grow less and less as they become more woman and man.

Both Beth and Jonathan need to know what they can share and what they cannot, how they are joined and how they are not. And Frances and I, as grown women and lesbians coming more and more into our power, need to relearn the experience that difference does not have to be threatening.

When I envision the future, I think of the world I crave for my daughters and my sons. It is thinking for survival of the species—thinking for life.

Most likely there will always be women who move with women, women who live with men, men who choose men. I work for a time when women with women, women with men, men with men, all share the work of a world that does not barter bread or self for obedience, nor beauty, nor love. And in that world we will raise our children free to choose how best to fulfill themselves. For we are jointly responsible for the care and raising of the young, since that they be raised is a function, ultimately, of the species.

Within that tripartite pattern of relating/existence, the raising of the young will be the joint responsibility of all adults who choose to be associated with children. Obviously, the children raised within each of these three relationships will be different, lending a special savor to that eternal inquiry into how best can we live our lives.

Jonathan has had the advantage of growing up within a nonsexist relationship, one in which this society's pseudo-natural assumptions of ruler/ruled are being challenged. And this is not only because Frances and I are lesbians, for unfortunately there are some lesbians who are still locked into patriarchal patterns of unequal power relationships.

These assumptions of power relationships are being questioned because Frances and I, often painfully and with varying degrees of success, attempt to evaluate and measure over and over again our feelings concerning power, our own and others'. And we explore with care those areas concerning how it is used and expressed between us and between us and the children, openly and otherwise. A good part of our biweekly family meetings is devoted to this exploration.

As parents, Frances and I have given Jonathan our love, our openness, and our dreams to help form his visions. Most importantly, as the son of lesbians, he has had an invaluable model—not only of a relationship—but of relating.

In talking over this paper with Jonathan and asking his permission to share some pieces of his life, I asked him what he felt were the strongest negative and the strongest positive aspects for him in having grown up with lesbian parents.

He said the strongest benefit he felt he had gained was that he knew a lot more about people than most other kids his age that he knew, and that he did not have a lot of the hang-ups that some other boys did about men and women.

And the most negative aspect he felt, Jonathan said, was the ridicule he got from some kids with straight parents.

"You mean, from your peers?" I said.

"Oh no," he answered promptly. "My peers know better. I mean other kids."

Volley with My Son

Judith Steinbergh

Once again we are at it
whacking the frail basket
of the birdy through the air,
the fourth June we have stretched
the sagging net across our yard
to be where honeysuckle leaks out
into the thickening dusk,
where roses are so profuse.
We are getting better, each year
the birdy sneaks through the net
fewer times, thwacks the wooden
frame of the racket less, swooshes
then hesitates in air, the way
it should, like a gull considering
a glint under the sea. We reach,
run, smack, talk of Plato, Sophocles,
where they converged and disagreed,
how Alexandre, beloved soldier,
loved a man, our eyes steadily
on the birdy, we do not let it drop,
how tough and tender he was, we
know we will jinx the volley if
we even mention it's been going on,
the trick here is to attend with
the sight to one thing and with
the mind to the other and both,
then will fly, will fly.

The Intolerable Burden of Loss

Minnie Bruce Pratt

In the *New York Times* photo, a young blonde woman sits staring, stunned. She holds up a large photograph of her cherubic, smiling little boy. At first this looks like a moment with which everyone sympathizes: when a mother publicly grieves her child killed in a tragic accident or lost in a nightmare kidnapping. But in this photo something jars slightly; there is no father next to the mother; her companion is a woman. And the caption reads: "A Virginia court's decision to remove a child from his mother because of her lesbianism is stirring controversy. Sharon Bottoms, left, lost custody of her 2-year-old son, Tyler Doustou, to her mother." At that moment perhaps the viewer's sympathy wanes, or turns to animosity.

But I know her look, I've sat in that desolate place, I've had my children taken from my arms, and felt that my children were almost dead to me, because I could not hold them or touch them. I had two boy children who I saw emerge, bloody and beautiful, from my body. I nursed them at my breast, I bathed their tiny perfect bodies and changed their diapers. I spooned them babyfood spinach, I taught them how to tie their shoes. I rocked them through earaches and bad dreams, I drove them to their first day in kindergarten. Then suddenly when they were five and six, when I fell in love with another woman and left my marriage to live as a lesbian—suddenly the world looked at me and saw an unfit mother. Suddenly my husband had legal grounds to take my children away from me and never let me see them again.

Like Bottoms, I was also a "somewhat immature and undisciplined, though loving mother,"—after all, we were both mothers at 21, barely out of girlhood. Like Bottoms I was an "irregular job holder"—finishing a Ph.D. in English literature. When I applied for teaching positions, the male interviewers would inquire, "How will you arrange child care? Are you planning to have more children? What will your husband do if we hire you?" And they never did.

But the standard for my being a "good mother" was not my parenting ability or financial stability. After all, my husband, a father at 23 and an unemployed graduate student, was no more mature in his role than

I was in mine. No, I was a young, immature and unemployed woman, but I was considered a fit mother as long as I was married and loyal to the man who was my husband. As soon as I asserted my independence, as soon as I insisted that my body was my own, as soon as I began a life in which I claimed the human right to form intimate social and sexual relations with whomever I chose, but specifically with other women—then I was seen to be a perverted, unnatural woman—by my husband, my mother, the people of the town I lived in, and the legal system. The letter from my husband's lawyer said he was seeking custody because of my "unorthodox ideas about the place of the father in the home"—my heresy consisted of disagreeing with the idea that men were superior to, and should govern, women.

Though over 15 years have passed between my agony at losing my children, and that of Sharon Bottoms, the issues remain the same. This is true despite the fact that I lost custody of my boys to my ex-husband, their biological father, and Sharon has, at least for now, lost her boy to her mother, the child's biological grandmother who sued for custody. But the reason for denying us our children was the same: simply the fact that we were in lesbian relationships. In the words of Judge Parsons who ruled in Henrico County Circuit Court against Sharon: "The mother's conduct is illegal and immoral and renders her an unfit parent." Illegal because in Virginia (and over twenty other states and the District of Columbia) sodomy, the "crime against nature" of lesbians and gay men, is still illegal. And the 1987 U.S. Supreme Court, in *Bowers v. Hardwick*, actually stated in majority opinion that it was maintaining the illegality of sodomy because that particular set of justices considered this kind of sex immoral, based on "traditional values."

By this logic, the "fitness" of a mother is determined, not on her ability to be a loving parent, but on her willingness to transmit traditional notions of rigid gender roles, sexual behavior, and cultural hierarchy to her child. Sharon Bottoms, as a lesbian in a committed relationship with another woman, is perceived as less fit to parent than her mother whose live-in boyfriend for 17 years was a man who, according to Sharon, sexually abused her twice a week during her teen years. Under the law and in the eyes of many people, Sharon's mother is more fit to mother because she endorses heterosexuality as an institution and female subservience as a tradition, and presumably will pass these values along to her grandson. This arrangement is seen as being in the child's "best interests."

But should we not ask what kind of damage will be done to a boy if his sense of self depends on dominating another person? Should we not inquire about the immorality of teaching a child that love can only occur with state-sanctioned approval, no matter how prejudiced the traditions of the state?

Much was made in the courtroom of the fact that Sharon's child calls her lover and partner "Dada." In most two-partner lesbian families the children call one woman Mama or Mom or Mother, and the other woman some different maternal variation, or perhaps by her given name. But in hostile legal circumstances, these women lose custody of their children anyway, despite a naming that affirms traditional female gender roles. Sharon Bottoms could be challenged for custody no matter what her child called April, her partner.

However, the word "Dada" evokes a truth about lesbian parenting that opponents violently condemn—two women who raise children in a home together challenge the very idea that gender roles, or gender expression, are irrevocably matched to biological gender. If a woman can "father," then perhaps she will pass on to the child the idea that a woman can live her life, in work, in recreation, even in the way she dresses, anywhere on the spectrum of feminine to masculine. Perhaps she will convey to a boy that he might be able to live his life any way, feminine to masculine, that he felt comfortable. Opponents of lesbian/gay parenting often present the "damage" to the child as a danger of him or her "becoming" gay. But this is only part of a larger fear that no matter what sexuality the child develops, the child might learn that rigid gender roles are not required. The child might learn the joy of possibility that comes when biological gender does not have to match socially-mandated gender in jobs or thoughts or love.

Psychiatric specialists testified for Sharon by outlining studies that showed no noticeable difference between children reared in lesbian and in heterosexual households. Nevertheless, Judge Patterson concurred with Sharon's mother's belief that the child would be "mentally and physically harmed" by the lesbian relationship; he stated there was a strong possibility that the boy would carry "an intolerable burden" for the "rest of his life." Sharon can see the child on Mondays and Tuesdays but not in her own home, nor in the presence of her lover.

By my divorce settlement ("And lucky to get it!" my lawyer said) I was forbidden to have the boys in my home if I shared the house with *any* other person; I could take them out of their home state only if we went to be with my mother, who my husband had threatened to call as a character witness for *him*. To see my boys sometimes I drove round-trip on three-day weekends, 14 hours nonstop there, 14 hours nonstop back. The youngest boy wrote in his school journal how he wished he could be with me more; the oldest boy talked to me late at night, long-distance phone calls, about his depression, about how sometimes he just wanted to die. I loved them, I called them, I saw them as much as I had time and money to do, we got through their baby years, preadolescence, teen years. When I finally said to the oldest, "What effect do you think my being a lesbian had on you?" he said, "None. I think my personality was most shaped by not having you with me as a mother all those years, by having you taken away from me."

It is ironic that Sharon Bottoms' case is being tried in Virginia, a state that enforced its law against racial intermarriage as late as 1967, until in *Loving vs. Virginia* the U.S. Supreme court finally declared this unconstitutional. The "miscegenation" laws codified not just the prejudices of white Southerners, but also the determination of a ruling elite to keep white and Black folk separate and unequal—and competing for jobs at ever lower wages. The determined political struggle of the African-American community, in the courts and in civil rights battles in the streets, abolished all such laws. In 1976, when I fought for custody of my children in Fayetteville, North Carolina, as I struggled to live as a self-reliant woman, not dependent, not submissive, the tide of women's liberation was rising through the South. Women were beginning to challenge an economic system that uses the threat of competition between the sexes as a way to limit working people's wages, benefits, and job conditions. Now with cases like that of Sharon Bottoms, the lesbian and gay community is fighting to end other inhumane limits on how all of us can live and love. And now we have allies, like Sharon's ex-husband, Dennis Doustou, who asked to testify for her and who says, "Tyler means the world to her."

In 1976 when I went to a lawyer for help in my struggle for my children, he said to me, "The world is not ready for someone like you." Can we say now, in 1993, that we are ready for someone like Sharon Bottoms, just an ordinary woman, a part-time grocery clerk trying to raise a child on not enough money, but with the love and support of another woman who cares about both of them? Let us declare, finally, that we are ready for this ordinary extraordinary woman who is saying to us, with her life, that to guarantee her right to be a lesbian and a mother is to take one more step toward liberation for *all* of us.

210

"We need places for people to learn the lessons of gender and race and culture and their own humanity. It's tempting to use that African proverb that says it takes a whole village to raise a child. Because the real problem goes far beyond the question of raising feminist sons and daughters. Our villages are not whole. It's not just our individual families that are in trouble. And until we can figure out a way to reeducate ourselves, rediscover the essence of community and redefine ourselves as neighbors and as friends, our children will continue to reflect our confusion and denial through the prism of their own frustration, until we barely recognize them as our own."

—Johnetta B. Cole, interview in Ms., 11/93

Laura Hamilton with her partner and twin sons.

Raising Sons with Emotion

Laura Hamilton

I guiltily dream of daughters, with my twin sons sleeping in the room above me. I ache for some imagined bliss of the union between related women. I crave the unique closeness I know gender provides and I yearn to nurture a being with whom I can intuitively connect. Yet these sons are so dear, entirely whole and perfect, and I look over my shoulder as the thoughts come to mind.

I do acknowledge the reality of chasms between mother and daughter. I recognize the inherent pitfalls in that bond I long for, the danger and risk in the very relationship that offers a healing force unlike any I seem to be able to manufacture for myself. I long to explore my path and review my journey in the company of a girl child. To wander farther myself, while watching her clamber over the path of her own making, appears so comforting from here. To have been in the company of a mother myself at those moments of facing sheer cliffs or jagged crevasses seems magical to me.

In parenting this pair of boys, I feel both cramped and stretched beyond my limits. I worry that my feminism and emotional base are too strong for their fledgling masculine selves. I am proud as well as concerned that they are too close to their feelings. They have emotional reactions to things I sometimes believe they "should" take in stride though I also know this is normal for them.

I fear the depth of tenderness that one of the boys at seven lavished on his stuffed bunny. Torn between protecting his instinctive parenting and fear of ridicule from the "regular" world, I carefully asked if he was sure he wanted to bring it to the park. Watching him push "Bob" on the swings brought tears to my eyes.

Now at eleven my son has to handle unthinkingly astonished questions from the librarian when he asks for books on knitting and quilting. I want to scream at her sexism or sit her down to explain how similar to Legos it is, how much logic, math and patterning it involves as well as the creative pleasure and sensory satisfaction in using yarn and fabric to make something all his own. He is entitled to all this, obviously, and yet I too hesitate sometimes when he asks if he should bring it along to the beach. Someone will make fun of his choices some day; do I prepare him for that?

Yet I am glad that they cry and choose their friends so carefully. I delight in their empathy and their awareness of the intuitive and unspoken dialogue. I was raised in a gender-biased society, however, and at times I admit that I cringe and compare them to "regular boys" with frogs and jackknives in their pockets, not poems and beads to string. I love their connection with and need for creativity and conversation.

Where will they find acceptance and companionship? Have I skewed their natural maturation by my passions? Do I really have that much influence?

The love between my sons and me will never disappear. I am more sure of that than any truth I have found. And yet increasingly we speak two different languages. We communicate amazingly well considering that fact; love and gesture go a long way but I can see them drifting into a haze of adolescent maleness, to places I wouldn't choose to visit even if I could. They show the pain and loneliness as they look back at me sometimes. I'm sure my loss and hurt shows too, the silent ache that throbs when I am closest to them.

My very feminist aunt once told me that changes in society were up to women like me who were raising sons to be nonviolent in the face of persistent messages from the patriarchy. I feel overwhelmed by the task. This is more responsibility than I ever bargained for. I need to be sure I am not raising batterers or rapists. Even more, there are moments when I hope I am raising kind and caring male role models who feel secure enough in their sense of self that other, younger men may someday be shaped by their gentleness and quiet strength.

But what if I am wrong? What if my efforts to break the mold result only in forming two young men who feel out of place in every group, who are isolated and solitary creatures and because of rejection and their resulting anger lash out in crazy and unpredictable ways? Can I live with that? Do mothers of baby girls whirl endlessly like this, banging themselves against the edges of What If?

So I dream. If she arrived, I'm aware that she might drive me wild with wishes for Barbie dolls, exasperate me with her long nails and eyeshadow and then worry me with unsuitable lovers; but she would be my own kind in a certain immutable way. As I fret the years away over these boys, I dream of a daughter.

The Macho Feminist

Victoria Alegria Rosales

Though each of us may define feminism differently, my own definition is that part of being a feminist is not to hurt nature.

Xavier doesn't even know that he is a feminist man as he teasingly shows me his muscles, trying to overpower me in arm wrestling. He's 6'2", 190 pounds. I'm 5'4", 160 pounds. As he challenges me to fight him back, he tells me about his latest booking at the Las Vegas jail. As he says "pigs," Xavier's mouth fills with angry saliva, the same kind he must have used to spit on the police car that hauled him to jail.

"I hate this town. Every time I get off the ship, the pigs are after me," he tells me. "They smell money."

That was two years ago. Last year he got married to a woman who refuses to move out of Las Vegas. And true, when Xavier gets off the ship, he has lots of cash with him for having worked on oil rigs like the Exxon Valdez, although he refused to work on that particular ship.

I'm Xavier's natural mother. When he was ten I gave up custody of him in order to get off welfare. Next time I saw him, he was a teenager with braces. I had to send him back to his father because I didn't have the money to take him to an orthodontist.

After my giving up custody, his dad wanted to keep sleeping with me but I refused. His dad and wife got even with me by adopting him without my consent, cutting off all visitation rights. I was too much of an immigrant to realize what this meant. After Xavier's father got what he wanted from his second wife, he left her. Then he married his wife's best girlfriend. So, Xavier has had two other mothers besides me. He's closest to me, though.

Maybe he remembers the antiwar marches I took him to while I was attending UC Riverside. Perhaps he hasn't forgotten the rallies in the mall for cleaner air, or the movies we attended, like *Panama Deception*. Xavier has gone many times through the canal. Once he commented about the struggles of the natives fighting the U.S. Government. "As the ship goes by, they throw stones at us," he excused himself. "I feel ashamed. But I'm only half American, right?"

I just listen. I am certain that Xavier still remembers our bike rides because we didn't have the money for gasoline for the big Buick, the only possession his father left. So what did it matter if we hardly ate from one day to the next—beans, tortillas and rice? Weren't we trying to save Riverside from becoming another polluted city like Los Angeles?

If you were to ask Xavier if he is a feminist, he would deny it. "Me, a feminist? Nawww." Then pointing or hugging me by the shoulders, "My mom here is." But in his heart of hearts, Xavier is a feminist.

Today, I am in a Las Vegas apartment complex which has an American flag at the entrance. I have come to meet my granddaughter before Xavier ships out again.

Xavier, his wife, their new baby girl Sherry, and I are sitting down in front of the TV. Xavier is waiting anxiously to see the movie about the Exxon Valdez disaster.

"Why do you want to see that movie?" I ask, thinking about the thousands of birds, fish, mammals and vegetation that had to die because of the greed of an oil company.

"I could have been on that ship," he tells me, eyes glued to the TV. Sherry burps on his shoulder. His wife had just breastfed her.

"Look what you did!" he gently scolds, as he wipes his shoulder and the baby's mouth.

"What happened?" I asked curiously, wanting to know more about why he refused the job with Exxon.

"Couldn't ship out from Frisco," he tells me as he gets up to turn on the volume. "Responded to an ad, offering jobs in Alaska—was flown to Houston and offered a non-union job."

"Who's in Houston?"

"Exxon Headquarters."

"So you didn't take the job?"

"Naww. Met the crew. Didn't want to work with a bunch of assholes who didn't know shit from the ground," he pronounces "assholes" with the same disgust he would call someone a "scab."

Xavier's Indian ancestry from his Cherokee grandfather mixed with my Mexican blood makes him look darker and meaner. I can see why the cops hassle him. Right now his profile looks like that of a true Indian Viking ready to smash at the injustice of the oil companies.

"I'm happy you didn't take the job," I say during a commercial.

"Me, too," he spits through the corner of his mouth.

216

"But what about if you had been forced to work to feed Sherry?" I inquire. "Don't you think many of those men had to do it to feed their families?"

"Yeah, but Exxon could afford sending them to school the way my union sent me to Maryland."

"Couldn't you have done something?"

"Me? Against all those goons? Naww. Those men have no hearts. If I had worked for them, I'd be in jail now. Could you have bailed me out?"

"No," I say, honestly.

"See? Last year bail cost me a few grand," Xavier tells me, lowering the volume of the TV.

I stop watching TV to take a bath. The sight of birds and otters bathed in oil has made my body feel as if I myself am covered with that gook. When I return, I notice there's a tear in Xavier's eye. Yes, when I was in the bathroom I cried myself, for all the animals that were asphyxiated in that oil.

Every once in a while, Xavier still blames me for giving him up to his father. I think he has never understood my need to break with tradition—my need to serve myself and not a man. But in other ways Xavier understands about my love relationships with women better than my own family. However, when he gets angry, he reminds me how glad he is that he grew up with his Dad in a middle-class environment. To add to the insult, he says, "If you had raised me, I may have become a cholo or a car thief." Do you remember all the candy I used to steal from the stores?"

"Yes," I snap in retaliation, knowing he is just kidding. "That's why I sent you to live with your Dad. But remember, I gave you the choice!"

"Yeah. But I was only ten. I couldn't decide for myself."

Since Sherry's birth, Xavier hopes that we will become a family once more. To prove his intentions, he passes Sherry to me as his wife's eagle eye watches me. I cuddle Sherry in my arms as I used to do with Xavier. His wife goes and locks herself into the bedroom as she always does. Xavier has told me how disappointed she is in my lifestyle. Yesterday her relatives came and she locked herself with them in the room. I went and opened the door and introduced myself.

"Ah, we know who you are, señora," said the man in the group in Spanish. "Xavier showed us a video of you."

Xavier's wife is afraid I might contaminate their child with my liberalism, my ideals, and my feminism. I try very hard to keep my mouth shut. Why did he marry this Mexican woman, I wonder. Is he trying to find me through her? I never was as Catholic as she. She is angry because I said it was a waste of money to marry in the church. "Why don't you use your money to take a trip instead?" I had suggested. "The Pope doesn't need your money."

I never had a crucifix either on top of my bed. Nor did my family ever force us to go to church. She must be pissed because we didn't go to church on Sunday when Xavier took me out, I think, hugging Sherry's little body. She is making all kinds of funny noises with her mouth.

"Dear Sherry," I whisper in her ear. "You must feel very proud of your macho, feminist daddy because he didn't have anything to do with the worst environmental disaster in humankind."

Sherry answers me with a big yawn, making her hands into fists. I think about all the arguments I am going to have with her mother. I am still fighting with my own mother for not understanding my feminism. Oh well, I'll know how to defend her from her mom.

In my farewell to my granddaughter I promise to tell her more about her Daddy. Next time I come to visit, I won't forget to tell her about how much her Daddy loves to feed the seagulls, and about all the fights he gets into with his buddies on the ship, when they throw glass or hot pepper wrapped in meat to the birds, thinking it is funny.

The Age of Reason

Mary Kay Blakely

The young boy thrives in the limelight of family attention and affection. Three of his most steadfast cheerleaders—three familial fans—are gathered around the kitchen table for a supper celebration.

He's 7 today. Seven. The age of reason.

His head bobs up and down in the waves of his intemperate glee. Instinctively, I survey the landscape of his head, searching around the crown for the familiar cowlick that sends the hair in all directions.

The nurse is holding a mirror between the stirrups. "See! Can you see it! The head's crowning!" I see the swirling mass of hair, spinning strands, drawing me deeply into the mirror, into the rushed beginnings, the unstoppable contractions, the contradictions of motherhood. I know that spot. The mental snapshot I took seven years ago at 4:15 a.m., that most kissed place on the crown of his head.

We clear the dishes and he breaks open the box of birthday candles, counting the waxy spirals to the magic number. "Know what 5 plus 2 is, Mom? Same as 3 plus 4!" He smiles at me with new-math wisdom.

How can he be 7? We're both still getting used to the bonds of motherhood, still jockeying for position in the me and he of it. The job of my longest tenure, mothering—the state of semisurprise, semidelight, semiconfusion. When can I expect to be accustomed to motherhood if not after seven years?

The smile spreads over the tiny acreage of his freckled cheeks, a smile contagious up to his brow, a smile deliberately intended to charm the susceptible mother at the table. It works. It works just fine.

I pass the picture of him on the breakfront every day, returning the chuckle I read on his face. It's a private joke between us, the kaleidoscopic pleasure of knowing each other.

He pokes the candles through the thick chocolate frosting on the top of the cake. There's a calculated clumsiness in his actions—he has to pause after each one to lick his fingers. Seven delicious executions of candle planting.

The personality is permanently formed in childhood. All things shaped and molded—by SEVEN? Little psyches firmly in place? Before he can read the

Bhagavad Gita? Before he can argue the Constitution? Before he can comprehend what Simone de Beauvoir meant? Before he has fallen in love/gone to war/left home? No. More shaping and molding to come. Much more. Outside my influence.

The cake is placed on the table for the opening ceremony, its iced surface now a relief map of fingerprints, with a small population of teetering candles, the intoxicating symbols of a developing life.

This is the boy the man will come from. Will I like—no, will I love—the man the way I love this boy? The forthcoming man. A vague fear of him. The maleness that threatens to separate us.

I have yet to face the understandable panic in my friend's last letter, the sentence jumping off the page like a banner headline: "Number one son sprouted pubic hair this summer!" She, caught between her class-action anger at men and her wild devotion to her two young sons. "How do I talk to him now? How will I know when to knock on his door?" The mother and young man exchange places of power, in accordance with custom, in recognition of the status of "man." Is detachment inevitable?

His dad places a modest pile of presents in front of him, still wrapped in the brown bags they were brought home in. This boy, the son of two working parents, doesn't know that children usually celebrate their birthdays with homemade cakes shaped like giraffes and presents of primary colors and complicated bows. This boy knows only parcel-post brown and cellophane tape.

In 20 years, in his group-therapy sessions, what will his "unhappy childhood" stories be? He asked for a cap gun. Nobody got him a cap gun. Nobody would. "Vous travaillez pour l'armeé, Madame?"—"You are working for the army, Madame?" a Frenchwoman asked the poet Adrienne Rich, learning that she was the mother of three sons. There are things he wanted, he will tell the therapist, that we didn't give him. A gun. What else?

His face reflects the disciplined excitement of an experienced gift-getter, holding the mirth back behind the dike of the wrapping paper. I memorize him with a gulping, hungry, mother gaze: the distractingly tweakable cheek, the huggable head, the body so perfect. The boy, increasingly, commands a private space around him, a space that even needy mothers may not trespass. No tweaks on the cheek without his permission now, as he claims more territory for himself.

The regret and the pride, the teeter-totter of relentless motherhood. What will the man-child do with his independence: Will he become "such a man as our daughters, born and unborn, will be pleased to live among," like the poet Audre Lorde describes, the kind of man who understands that "women do not exist to do his feeling for him?"

Or will he be an exasperating man, one who wears women out with expectations and resistance? Will this man-child have an invitation to the promised land of women's affections and respect?

Finally, the wrappers give way under his insistent probing and his laugh rolls out uncaged from the strain of young impatience. The prize at the bottom of the Cracker Jack box is a large spaceship—clearly a boy toy, clearly the gift of parents aiming to please. Clearly a compromise—he'll defend it, no doubt, with imaginary cap guns and unloaded index fingers.

This, the age of reason. I want a truce called in the battle of the sexes, the possibility of reasonableness on the threshold of his manhood. I met a young man of such reasonableness, a rare young man in a class I taught once. He seemed to absorb the meaning of the women students without needing to translate their native language into his own image, without retreating from their anger, without defensiveness. In his journal he likened the class discussions to a campfire circle of intimate friends. He felt privileged to be in their confidence. He "wanted to please them," he wrote, because he "enjoyed the company of the women." He thought they were marvelous, these women who were becoming his friends, in their rawness, in their realness, their rowdiness. This young man, I thought when I read his journal, has a very good chance of learning to love women.

We lit the candles on the cake, the boy's face a flashcube of happiness. Looking at him, capturing the candid range of expressions, there are no amendments I wish to make to the boy of 7, so magnificent are his raw materials. I want to light more candles for him without extinguishing any of these.

I wish I could wrap up the formula for him, to become a man "our daughters would be pleased to live among." A man who would "enjoy the company of the women." A man who would earn the privilege of their respect. I wish I could give him the Promised Land for his birthday, an invaluable gift for a man-child arriving at the age of reason.

He was pleased with himself when he blew out the candles. And then we sang him a song.

What about the Boys?

Anna Quindlen

The eighth grade boys were not happy campers the day I came to call. "Why don't you ever write about the sexual harassment of men?" one of them asked darkly. "Why don't you ever write about men being raped?" Well, I said, one answer is obvious: men have plenty of troubles, but they are not always identical to those of women.

Looking back on Take Our Daughters To Work Day, and the inevitable and considerable backlash on the subject of boys, the same thought crosses my mind. The women who cooked up this idea believed there was something important we needed to communicate to our daughters about their worth in the world. Boys need to learn many things about themselves, too. But they are different things than girls need, addressed in a different fashion.

The consciousness-raising groups of 20 years ago led to a great social revolution, but it sometimes seems to me that we raised the consciousness of only half the people. Child care continues to be seen as a woman's issue; domestic and sexual violence are omnipresent. At Tailhook there were T-shirts that said "Women Are Property." The great changes of the women's movement did not ultimately change the hearts and minds of many men in some of the ways we women had hoped.

Take Our Daughters To Work Day was about the hearts and minds of little women. The girls at our office put out a newspaper called *Girls' Times*, and they quoted Marie Wilson, president of the Ms. Foundation for Women, saying we wanted girls to feel "visible, valued and heard."

In other words, they were made to feel important. There were hundreds of them at *The Times*, and they humanized the work environment, presto-changeo. "Feels kind of lonely without the girls here," one man said next day in the elevator.

The next day I got a lyrical letter from Elizabeth Lyman Packer, whose father, Lauren D. Lyman, won the Pulitzer Prize in 1936. She described a trip to the *Times* newsroom with her father when she was 11 years old, the black and white of her dress—"like the *Times* itself"—the gray of the copy paper, the black of the typewriters.

They set her byline—LIBBY LYMAN—in metal type. "Everyone was kind to me, all the men, only men," she wrote. But more than half a century later, her memories were bittersweet, too: "Maybe now I am realizing I was seeing a world that would never be for me, or more than that, it would never occur to me that I might be a part of it." Our business lost a fine writer when Libby Lyman counted herself out.

What about the boys? people kept asking last week. And I understood the concerns, because one of the greatest challenges I face as a mother is bringing up feminist sons. If 20 years from now the guys still don't get it, we will still be struggling, at work and at home. If I raise two retro princes with corked-up emotions to hand down to some newer version of my younger self, it will be a great failure, for me and for them.

But the simple fact is that no one has to assure her sons that a boy can grow up to be President, or to teach them that little trick of holding your keys just so to jab out the eyes of a rapist. Girls wonder how you juggle work and family; boys figure they'll do it by getting married. We still start from different places.

I know lots of boys felt left out last week. And I know lots of boys in poor communities feel left out permanently, of the work force, of the mainstream, just like their sisters do.

But maybe some boys learned something about a different place on Wednesday, learned what it is like to feel overlooked because of your sex. My fourth grader had to write an essay about how he might feel if he were a girl, and his empathy level was pretty high. So far, so good.

When I look at some of the men I meet, it seems that what they needed to learn when they were boys isn't to be found at the office. It's an interior world, of intimacy, of connection. It's a world in which being a father is as important—and as time-consuming—as being a mother, and the most pressing business of our lives is our relationships.

I'm not sure if you can distill those needs down to a place, even the kind of largely symbolic place that the work world was for girls last week. Take Our Sons Home isn't right. Take Our Sons To Their Feelings is too murky. There's no doubt that boys need a hand, too. But it's a different hand, a different way, to take them where they need to go.

Rosalind Warren with her son Tom.

How to Raise Your Son to Be a Homicidal Lesbian Terrorist

Rosalind Warren

My own belief is that any significant attempt to influence one's child to adhere to a particular belief system, feminism included, is doomed to failure. My husband, for example, was brought up by staunch Republicans and is now a liberal Democrat. I, who was raised by liberal Democrats, became a radical feminist. Raising my son Tom to be a radical feminist will no doubt result in his embracing Republicanism (shudder) when he reaches adulthood.

Nevertheless, one has to try.

It's not easy teaching a handsome little middle-class white boy to think like a feminist—everybody else is telling him that the world is his oyster; meanwhile we're telling him he has to share.

In teaching a young boy to become a feminist, it helps not to allow him to watch any television. In particular, beer commercials.

We taught Tom the word "sexist" at age two. Now, at four, he understands what it means, can recognize it when he sees it, and realizes that mom and dad don't think sexism is good. At times he tries to educate his peers, with mixed results.

Tom and I enjoy reading feminist literature together, which I hope will undermine the inevitable anti-feminist bias of the stuff they read to him in school. Tom's current favorite is Diane DiMassa's *Hothead Paisan, Homicidal Lesbian Terrorist*. It isn't 100 percent politically correct, but I like the humor and Tom really likes all the explosions.

Of course reading *Hothead* may well be undermining our attempts to raise Tom to become a pacifist. But that's another story...

Katherine Keefer and sons Eli and Aaron.

Raising Aaron

Katherine Keefer

In the end I don't know who raised whom. He, however, had it figured out at the age of 5. "I should have been the Mom," he said. It was true, he was far more practical than I. He still is. He was born a screamer and it wasn't until his brother, a non-screamer, was born that I realized he came that way and it wasn't my doing. This was an amazing revelation. I stopped trying to make him happy and started trying to help him get along in the world.

He was happily into destroying Tonka trucks when his brother Eli was born. He was two and he told me later I wasn't strict enough. He watched his brother's every move, and I watched for flying blocks. But he drew a picture and pinned it low on the wall, for Eli, he said. He used to make up stories about everything he saw. The sunlight in the bushes was the broken moon. Mr. Thunder and Mr. Lightning would visit him at night in his bed.

We left his dad, the three of us, when he was four. We left in an old Chevy station wagon. Sometimes it got stuck in second and you had to pull over and lift the hood and unstick it. We talked a lot about what is unseen, unspoken, and he was always good about knowing. I would say, "What's really bothering you?" and he would stop crying to tell me.

Until he started kindergarten he was called by his middle name, Trout. I asked him as we were walking to school the first day, "Do you want to be Aaron or Trout?" Without hesitation he said Aaron. Sometimes I miss my Trout but it may be just as well because Eli called him Shout and that was a little too close to the truth.

In the first grade he took dance classes and fell in love with his teacher. I wouldn't have a TV in our house but by the end of circle time at school he could talk the morning cartoons as if he'd seen them. I would ask his teacher, "How was he today?" "Oh, he's wonderful," she'd say. But the minute he'd hit the car he'd start screaming, "I can't be good another minute." "This isn't fair," I'd answer. Then I started bringing cheese and peanut butter to stuff in his mouth the minute I saw him.

Once he said, "The way I have it figured, Mom, if I have a football I can take to school, they will have to play with me because it's my football." Much later I learned that if I wanted his cooperation I had only to present him with the idea that it was the next logical step. "It must have been hard for you," I said later, "living with Eli and me." "Oh yes, Mom," he answered.

Most of my great child-rearing ideas disintegrated into whatever worked. And I am ashamed to say what ultimately worked, the bottom line, was the fact that I could get madder than he could. I don't think I ever yelled at his brother, but when I really wanted a behavior to end it worked until he got bigger than me.

I did tell them that there were two things they couldn't do, play Little League or join Boy Scouts, because they were paramilitary organizations and I did not raise them to be cannon fodder. There were other reasons as well: for one, I did not want to be a den mother and, two, baseball games are much too serious and unending. They did play pool after school at the Boys Club and became quite good. They also played soccer and I spent Saturdays standing in the rain watching them. They had bus passes and became quite independent. They stuck together, they always fascinated each other. At night they drew pictures and made up games.

We painted the walls of our house with murals of Wild Things and Star Wars. We listened to Bob Dylan. There was always art everywhere and the funny thing is neither of them ever broke a thing. And when I'd finish a piece and it wasn't quite right I'd say, "Aaron, what's wrong with this?" and he'd tell me. And he'd be right. I baked bread and every summer we made quarts of blackberry jam.

I never told them that the way they felt was wrong. I always told them I needed them to make our family work. I tried to give them jobs that made sense, like being in charge of the wood when we had only wood heat. I worked as an artist-in-the-schools and so when one of them was sick and I had to go teach, the other one would stay home to be company. We did a lot of things together. When they were six and eight my mother gave them ski equipment for Christmas, asking, "What kind of mother doesn't take her kids skiing?" They loved it, and I started working at the mountain on weekends.

Aaron idolized his father. When he was eight he would cry himself to sleep sobbing, "I just want to see my dad." His dad was a musician and would stop by Saturday evenings on his way to a gig. When I said, "The boys want to see more of you," he would reply, "Oh, they know I love them." I was furious. Aaron said, "Oh Mom, please don't get mad at Dad." I said, "Are you afraid he won't come at all?" "Oh yes," he said. His brother, on the other hand, was always looking for a dad. The only time I tried to be a family with a dad, Eli said, "He's not our style, Mom." Then he said, "Oh, I'm so sorry, I didn't mean that." "It's okay," I said, "You are absolutely right." He was, too, and besides the man drank too much.

I am convinced that when boys are about thirteen alien beings come down and inhabit their bodies and suddenly you don't know who your children are and neither do they. It is terribly strange to no longer know your own child. I started finding beer cans under Aaron's bed.

When Aaron got his driver's license, I handed him a set of keys to our only car and said, "Just ask me before you take it." Twenty hours later he had totaled it. "Mom, I'm so sorry," he said. "I know you loved that car." He was shaking, but within two days he was laughing, "Mom, it wasn't that bad." But I saw the car and I don't know how the kids walked away. I just wanted him alive.

I thought, well, he's learned to be more careful, but the following weekend he drove his grandfather's car off the side of the levee. I couldn't believe it, I was furious, and he was convinced it was just more bad luck. When he finally earned enough to get his own car, he handed me a set of keys. I was dumbfounded and incredibly touched.

I told a friend I was worried about him and she offered him an after-school job; he started delivering airline tickets for a woman-run travel agency. They adored him. I told him that I needed him to work to help pay for his own expenses, which was true, but I also didn't want him hanging out with his friends so much. They partied a lot, got stoned, dropped out of school, drove their cars too fast. I didn't know what to do. We got counseling and the counselor told me his friends were his business. That was hard, but I changed my attitude and he realized we could talk about things and I would be able to hear him.

When they were sixteen, I told them that if they wanted to live with their dad it was okay. I didn't want them to go but I would understand. And at the worst of our troubles I screamed, "If you can't obey my rules you need to live with your father." Aaron looked at me and, dead calm, said, "That's not playing fair, Mom." That was the last time we fought. The funny thing is he behaved perfectly for his father.

He is 21 now. It hit me suddenly how much he not only looked after his brother but me too. I said, "Thank you for taking care of me." Things got hard, I was tired, sometimes lonely, we moved a lot, broke always. There weren't many secrets, and we saw it through. I really don't know if I could have grown up or made it without them. They were my rock, my reason. Sometimes I feel bad that we moved so much. In ways it made us really close because we were always starting over and all we had was us, but there were a lot of tears too.

Now, Aaron is a fourth-year architecture student at the University of Oregon. Eli is a freshman at San Francisco State, a skateboarder and graffiti artist. He's a healer and when he smiles energy radiates out. He said to me when he graduated from high school, "Mom, I don't know if I want to go to another competitive four-year institution." "Well," I said, "then you need to get a job." "I don't see why it has to be an either/or choice," he said. I still grin when I think of it.

It is time now for them to take care of themselves. I tell them I want to know them, who they are, what they think, because I find them incredibly interesting.

A Tree, a House or a Car

Gail Rebhan

The whole family
is riding
in the car.
My six year old
is perplexed
by a song he heard
on Sesame Street.
The song says
that girls
can grow up to be
anything they want.
My son says
that is not true.
I brace
myself for
a sexist comment.
My husband and I
exchange glances.
Then my son says
that's silly,
girls can't grow
up to be

a tree,   a house   or a car.

I agree that
women can't be
those things.
But I reply
men can't be
those things
either. I know
responds my son.
I'm relieved.

Judith Arcana and son Daniel.

The Book of Daniel (an adaptation)

Judith Arcana

As the mother of a son, I recognize the frustration and pain of knowing that my child is at once of my body and alien to it; I live with the anxious understanding that my boy's life is not in my hands, that all I want for him must be wrested from the patriarchy that claims him. Though I made and fed him out of my flesh, I am now "other" than he.

My son Daniel was born October 27, 1971. The following are excerpts from a journal I kept in his first ten years.

February, 1976

Having Daniel—a son—in my life, in my house, has made me acknowledge the humanity of men. The beauty and possibility of good in him, as a baby, as a boy, make it impossible for me to leave off with men, to count them out. I have to see that they all were once this, this tender little person, this graceful little body—innocent of its phallic destiny, symbol of guns and hammers, rapes and beatings.

November 17, 1976

Last night I was singing to Daniel before he went to sleep. I was singing "On Top of Old Smokey," which I've been singing to him since he was born. I had gotten to the line about how "they'll hug you and kiss you and tell you more lies than cross-ties on a railroad or stars in the skies," when he stopped me, saying, "I don't want to hear that song. You hate men. You hate me. I'm a boy, and I'll be a man when I grow up. You hate what I'm going to be when I grow up."

Shocked into silence, I recovered and began to talk. I explained why I "hated" most men—as briefly and simply as I could lay out male supremacy to a five-year-old, using examples from our lives that he already understood, like men who cruise by and call out to women on the street. He seemed to be understanding, but what he wanted was reassurance, not politics. I told him there were some good men, and that he was good. We hugged and kissed, and I thought I'd done pretty well.

Early May, 1977

Daniel and I went shopping to buy him an umbrella. I knew, and he didn't, that there are people who say that boys shouldn't carry umbrellas, but I didn't tell him that. It turned out that the child-sized umbrellas were all in the girls' section. But they were with hats and gloves and stuffed animals, so he didn't notice. This was fortunate because Daniel's become careful about publicly using anything that is designated "for girls": even in a shoe store where the sneakers are all the same except for the color of the boxes(!), he can be turned aside by some fool of a salesman's saying, "Hey, tiger, those are girls' shoes; c'mon over here," pointing to the inevitably dark-blue something-or-other. So he looked through the umbrellas. Just as he chose the most beautiful one—it had a curved wooden handle and was made of thick poplin cloth in wide yellow, blue, pink and green stripes that blurred into a rainbow as he spun it on its point in the aisle—a saleswoman walked toward us wearing a disapproving face, but aiming it only at me. I hoped she would be decent about telling him not to spin the merchandise, but she sidled up to me and stage-whispered, "You know, that's a girl's..." Taken aback, but by now experienced, I cut her off: "We don't think umbrellas have any sex, and we're going to buy this one. He'll wear it home; thank you." Perhaps a bit too clipped, but I just can't be nice about it anymore.

Spring, 1978

Daniel says that he "won't listen to the bad men" who don't respect women. He says he "won't play with them." But he has already told me that he's afraid to talk back, tell off, or hit "a great big man," including his own father. Ever since he was a baby, strangers have spoken to him on the street and, almost as often, touched him. Men will pat his head or give him a mock punch on the shoulder, but never hear or try to hear what he actually says in response to them. It is true that women also touch him without permission, though they do not hit him or call him Butch or Tough Guy. We have spent a lot of time talking about what he can say or do when people use his body this way, and he seems to understand the correlation between his experience and men's use of women's bodies, the connection between women and children in a man's world. But he says that he just can't say anything to a man who uses him that way. "When it's a great big man, I'm too scared, Mom." We've got to be able to do something in these situations. One irony here is that some of these people—the ones who don't call him Butch—think he's a girl anyway. They're still saying, "But such curly blond hair!" and "such pretty blue eyes!" as if they'd never seen a boy or man who didn't look like Edward G. Robinson. But whatever sex they think he is, they think he's fair game. They start conversations with him, and then walk away or ignore him when he responds to their empty questions—"Would you like to come and live with me?" "Hey kiddo, do ya like to play ball?"

NOTE: Reading over that last entry called up the memory of one such blatant trick played on Daniel. There was an old woman next to us on a crowded bus. She may have been the one who kept giving him pennies to make him smile; maybe not. At any rate, after gazing at him for several minutes, she spoke to me. "What a beautiful little girl, so sweet!" Daniel looked up at her. "I'm not a little girl; I'm a little boy." "Ohhh! How lucky! That's much better!" she replied. Now, maybe she was trying to be polite, thinking she had insulted him, knowing what an insult it is to call a boy a girl. She was absolutely sincere. She really believed that it was "much better" to be a boy, and though in many ways, especially from her point of view, she may have been right, in more ways, especially from my point of view, she was wrong. What a puzzle for the little boy to figure out. Was it better to be a boy? How? What made it better? And how did that woman feel, then, since she was obviously not a boy? And how did I feel, also not a boy? Well, I just couldn't take on that lady on the bus. Later, because I couldn't help myself, I talked to Daniel about it, but he wasn't interested enough for me to make any positive impact, and I gave up. I wondered about his response, though. Did he say "I'm not a girl" because he was insulted? Or was he just trying to state his case, make his identity clear?

August 9, 1978

Today Daniel came home from camp and began to tell me a joke about a farmer's daughter whose father "stuffs razor blades up her pussy to hurt these guys when they do it with her. The three guys are American, Indian, and Polish." I hardly know where to begin. Fortunately, this happens on a day when I am so exhausted that I haven't the energy to get hysterical, so I behave calmly while I explain. This takes a long time, covering—as it must—not only women, sex, fathers and daughters, racism, profane/pornographic language, and the telling and hearing of such jokes by men and boys, but also an explanation of why, really, this "joke" isn't funny, even to him. Which he took in readily, having wondered what was funny about it, all the while laughing with a bunch of other little boys. That may be why he rushed in right off the camp bus and began to tell it to me, almost before saying hello. Maybe he was mystified by the story, by the experience. Am I always going to be there afterward? Will I continue to be willing to explain? At some point, certainly when he's older, I'm going to really resent this. I'm going to want him to be able to smell it coming like I do, to sense what's wrong, and not to laugh—even at cost to himself. I'm going to want him to do something about it, and maybe crack the glue of his male bond in the process.

Spring, 1979

Omie and I took the kids to Cocina Mexicana for dinner when we picked them up. They were full of excitement and information about their day, both eager to tell us about it. As they talked, I saw this happen: Daniel interrupted Nelly—talked right over her to finish most of the explanations she started, and she let him do it; she subsided when he took it away. At one point, she picked up a fork to illustrate her talk; they were explaining "the purpose of observation in the scientific method." He took the fork right out of her hands, finished her sentence, and went right on. She let him do it. I was in that bad position of not knowing what Omie thought about all this. Did she see it and choose to let it go by? Did she not want to remonstrate with my child? Could I take it upon myself to stop them both and run it down? I was too unsure, and let it go by. Later, at home, I reconstructed the scene with Daniel, explained what I'd seen and told him what was wrong. I was careful to explain it as a dynamic, so that he didn't think I was blaming him for doing something to Nell. He understood but, again, at least half the impact is lost when I don't do it in the moment. Whatever interplay there could have been between him and Nelly is impossible to construct, and she alone could have really told him what it meant to her to be interrupted, to have the fork taken out of her hands—and why she was willing to do that, to be that way.

September, 1979

Daniel is worried. He's been listening to Holly Near singing "Fight Back," and putting it together with my self-defense classes—came with me twice, loved it—and understands that there is a problem here. "What will happen to me and Jonathan when the women fight back? Will you kill all the men, or put us in jail?" (Oh to be powerful enough to do that, let alone whether we'd choose it or not!) "What happens to us when you make what she says you're going to make?" I explained that what she says we're going to make is "a safe home," and that only men who oppose that would be shut out of the lives of the women who live there.

Then I told him about separatism, a concept that was new to him, and he was pretty interested. He understands that not all women are separatists—though his initial questions would seem to indicate a fear that the extreme position may ultimately have to be taken by all women. I cut the annual Michigan music festival for women for him—he should be grateful, if not complacent. Anyway, he knows I'm not a separatist; I'm not giving up my son for the women anymore than I am for the men.

February 6, 1980

Daniel needs a sense that being male is okay, even good, with the possibility of full humanity available. He needs models now—new models—and he needs more contact with the struggles of men who are changing their male identity. Maybe boys do need to be around men, especially in this society, where so much of what we are is based on assigned sex roles. But how to find the right men? Are there any? There must be—but can I advertise for them? And how can I get them to do it? Should mothers just send boys off, like in the old days, to the men's lodge? We can't; the men aren't prepared, aren't capable—or willing to accept the responsibility, even if they could do it. Mothers have to raise boys, not just four or six or ten years, but sixteen or twenty—well into sexual and cultural masculinity. How are we going to make the proper arrangements? It is, so far, *ours* to arrange.

Daniel needs the sense that I accept and love him in his maleness, not *despite* his maleness.

October 23, 1980

I walked from the shower to my closet to my dresser, reaching for some clothes; we were dressing to go out for dinner. Daniel said to me, "Why are you walking around with no clothes on?" I replied that I was not "walking around," but getting dressed. It was a brief interchange but indicated something going on there about nakedness, about my body. He looks at me, not sure if he should, interested—as we all are—but nervous. He'll be nine next week. What happens now? Let him see what a real woman's body looks like, instead of the unreal images the media project? But then I feel used. And I don't want him to respond to me sexually either. But would he, necessarily? After all, I loved to look at my mother's body and liked to cuddle with her, but didn't feel sexual about her. Is that a fair comparison? Is that even true? What about all the negative sanctions on lesbianism? But had I absorbed all that by the time I was nine? Maybe. I sure had by the time I was eighteen—but I still looked at naked women—and men—whenever I could.

Early January, 1981

Even though I never got a regular program going with other mothers of sons, the tiny group that got together to see that disappointing movie about adolescent male sexuality was exciting. And even though my vague plans about a boys group remain vague, I understand what I can do right now and what I can't. I can't make a boys group because I'm not a boy. But I have escalated my social/cultural commitment to Daniel, and have been able to handle that, though the money part gets tough sometimes. And when I'm sitting in the audience next to him, watching him watch women sing and play, I really think these tickets may be more important than the rent money. And I see one answer I've been seeking. There are many women like me, feminist and antisexist, raising sons and struggling against the patriarchy's claim on them—and we have to come together, mothers and sons, socially and culturally—for here are the peers and "older brothers"—these other sons of women like me, boys who struggle to be themselves, who question the expectations of male culture.

January 15, 1981

Daniel and I went to our first mother-son acting workshop. He loved it. I loved it. When we came home, we talked for half an hour, even though it was a school night and way past his bedtime. We were peers, we were friends who had taken this class together, and out of the work at hand we exchanged impressions. We're working together; we've gone outside of our family roles to relate to each other—lucky that we like each other when we do that. I bless the night this idea came to me.

February 25, 1981

The mothers of girls are coming to realize that the more time their daughters spend with girls—out of the company of boys—the stronger, smarter and healthier they are. Watching Omie realize this, knowing that she might send Nelly to an all-girl school, I want to cry, I want to scream: But what about *my* baby? What about my child, born in the same innocence, harboring no innate evil, desiring no malevolent power—struggling, in fact, not to take that place being held open for him in the hierarchy of male supremacy. What about my *boy*? Will you leave him behind? Will you leave him alone with the coaches, the hearty boy-o's of the history department, the math teachers who assume boys are interested but girls aren't?

Yes, you will; maybe you should. Protect and nurture those girls, shelter and strengthen them. Teach the young girls our history and challenge them with the gift of women's wisdom, their birthright. But, sweet Goddess, how we'll miss them, my son and I. How he needs the temperance of their presence, indisputable reminder of who they really *are*— in the face of the lies other boys and men will teach him about them.

March 16, 1981

I am trying to discontinue tucking him in at night, like walking him to the door in the morning. Both of these are attached to an emotional separation that I don't want, but I do want to stop the sense of waiting on him. I want the goodnights and the partings to be mutually expressed, to be flexible. I feel constrained; I can't stand the position I'm put in—waiting on him, waiting for him to be ready, always having to keep aware of his needs. It's different now; he's older. This is where it's different for mothers of sons. I turn into a waiting woman, waiting on a miniature man who's nine years old. This fits into the sex-role socialization pattern. Certain postures and situations arise that subordinate me, and I hate them.

Am I trapped? Can I release myself from the pattern without losing some measure, a good measure, of the sweetness and tenderness that is between us? Is there no way I can explain this to him, so that we can go on taking and giving comfort without my being *used*? I have to keep in mind that at nine, Daniel is having a hard time accepting responsibilities, giving up being a little kid, moving on to being a middle kid. He wants and needs *more* hugging and kissing lately, more time and attention, more thumb-sucking, etc. He seems to be trying to store up a bunch so he can leave this phase behind him, to get in a lot now and then go on. Like drinking a lot of cool water before going into a desert.

April 23, 1981

Daniel used the word *fag* today. He said he didn't really know what it meant, but I could tell that he did, and was too ashamed to admit it. I came down real heavy, because he's too old for me to let that go by. We've done this one before, some years ago, and it's time to go around again. I want him to see that the general use of that negative label for male homosexuals is the same as dyke or kike or nigger.

So I told him that it was an insult, and one that specifically affected men that we know, naming them. I had never before told that any specific man was gay, knowing how it could backfire, wanting him to know them well before labelling them with some yahoo word.

Daniel uses the word *lesbian* to mean any woman who seems woman-loving and woman-identified, who dresses for herself and not necessarily in fashion, who wears no makeup or brassiere. This results in his thinking many more women to be lesbians than say they are, and while that might be better than assuming everybody's straight as a stick, he needs a more sophisticated explanation, certainly a sense of the suffering and anger, sacrifice and pain, that lesbian women (and gay men) live with. Because he's beginning to learn about the persecution and oppression of Jews, and naturally experiences his understanding emotionally, maybe I should begin with Hitler's persecution of lesbian and gay people.

Funny how the major questions, about sex and death and reproduction, come around and come around again. They get asked or come up somehow every few years, every time with greater sophistication on his part, and a fuller explanation from me. The first time we talked about gay men was when he was four, when Sam and Donald stayed with us for a week. Daniel opened with, "How come Sam and Donald wear earrings? Men don't wear earrings." (Now mind you, these guys were wearing stuff like multicolored crystal clusters or dangling bunches of fruit in both ears, not your simple gold ring on one side, evoking dashing pirates of the Caribbean.) I said, "Well, Sam and Donald are men, and they are wearing earrings. So, men must wear earrings, 'cause here they are." He said, "Oh, yeah," and smiled. Simple.

October 27, 1981
Today he'll get out of school a bit early to meet me; we're going to see a Marx Brothers matinee—A *Day at the Races* and A *Night at the Opera*. At 4:10 p.m., ten years to the minute since he came out of my body, we'll be sitting in the dark with Harpo, Chico and Groucho. I wish they'd been with us in the delivery room.

So he'll celebrate presents and sweets—and being ten! I'll celebrate the memory of his small head between my thighs, and my domed stomach collapsing as his shoulders slide out.

"...It is absurd to think that women on the path of feminism wish to abandon their sons, emotionally or otherwise. Rather, the mother-son relationship—like all relationships— is undergoing revaluation, both in the light of the mother's changing relationship to male ideology, and in terms of her hopes and fears for her sons. If we wish for our sons—as for our daughters—that they may grow up unmutilated by gender roles, sensitized to misogyny in all its forms, we also have to face the fact that in the present stage of history our sons may feel profoundly alone in the masculine world, with few if any close relationships with other men."

—Adrienne Rich, *Of Woman Born*

Penelope Sky and sons.

How You Change the World

Penelope Sky

I'm patting the six-year-old dry after a shower. "You wanna hear a joke?" he asks. "Sure." Pause. "Never mind." "What do you mean, never mind? Tell me the joke." "That's okay." "No, come on, I want to hear it." "I have a feeling you might think it's sexist."

My kids were born in the early eighties. Both times, I wanted a girl. I had three brothers and no sisters, and I'd never been close to my mother. I dreamed of living for the first time with someone essentially like me. I assumed that my daughter would be born liberated because I was enlightened. I was confident that raising a girl into a strong independent woman would be a snap, but I could not imagine how to prevent a boy from becoming a narcissistic and manipulative man. It was also desirable socially to have a girl, at least in the feminist liberal intellectual counterculture in which I'd come of age. Girls were politically correct before the term was coined; no one would criticize a baby of course, but among my friends and in the feminist essays I read, the subject of sons was avoided. (That my world was not the real world soon became evident. When I stepped out with my dog and my newborn son, a neighbor came into the street to peer into my front carrier. "You're supposed to have a boy first," he said approvingly.)

I have never cried easily, but at dinner a week or so after my son was born I burst into tears. I hadn't been experiencing anything like postpartum depression; I rapturously adored my gorgeous child from the instant he finally fought his way free of my body, and I was exhilarated by my new identity. But that afternoon I passed a little waterfront park where a bunch of men and young boys were playing ball, and a premonition of loss engulfed me. I saw that as my son grew up, I would be cut out of his life automatically because of my gender. He would belong to other boys and to men. I would be on the outside. It broke my heart to see that I was destined to be rejected by the person I loved most in the world. This sudden sense of tragedy was the first shadow to fall across my new life as a mother. I sat at the dinner table and howled with grief

243

as though I were mourning a death, one already expert hand automatically rocking the cradle at my side.

When my first child was two I deliberately became pregnant. The first time, I had a baby partly because I was in love with his father; the second time, I had a baby partly because I was in love with my son. I knew that my children's father and I weren't going to make it as a couple, and I was afraid that if I were left alone with one child I would wreck his life with the intensity of my attention. When I was six months pregnant the kids' father and I separated; although he came back shortly before the birth of our second son, I knew the reunion wouldn't last. By the time the baby was six months old and his big brother just over three, I was a single parent.

The boys' father chose not to be closely involved with their lives. He didn't want the responsibility of shared custody, he rejected the idea of scheduled visitation, and he believes that because I initiated our breakup, he should not be obliged to pay child support. Although he lives in the same small town as we do, he doesn't keep track of such details as who his sons' friends or teachers or doctors are, or their shoe or clothing sizes, or how they're doing in school. But he surfaces from time to time to run the kids around for a few hours or to root at a ballgame. Our older son has suffered immense grief for the father he knew as an infant and toddler, holding on to his love for his dad despite the high cost; for a long time I thought he was hurting himself with his stubborn devotion, but now I see that he is demonstrating the spiritual value of unconditional commitment. Our younger son is ambivalent about his father, unwilling to reject him but unable to let him into his heart; he is extremely close to me.

When my second son was born, my midwife, who knew that I hoped for a girl, leaned over and whispered, "You know how we change the world? By *having male children*." She had two sons of her own, quite a bit older than mine, but I was outraged by her remark. I thought she was accepting male privilege and implying that we could carry on behind the scenes, getting what we want by manipulating men as women have always been accused of doing. Raising boys has shown me how deeply I misunderstood the woman who helped bring them forth.

I have pretty much abandoned my old habit of characterizing unhappy situations as merely *sexist*, or *racist*, or *classist*. One of these elements may always be present, but now I find it more useful to recognize that in unequal relationships one party is always the oppressor, the other the victim. For example, in my early days as an isolated single working parent I would often feel so overwhelmed that I would turn on my children almost viciously, shouting at them, flooding them with complaints, criticism, and demands for understanding, bewildering and terrifying them. In the end I would be overcome with self-loathing and beg their forgiveness. Even then I saw the parallel between my uncontrollable verbal and emotional violence toward my beloved children, and the syndrome of physical battery between a violent man and a dependent woman (I had served eighteen months on a crisis line for battered women). Now I understand that I felt victimized by my children and that I consequently rose to oppress them. I knew it was not their fault that I was so often on the brink of disaster. It was a long time before I understood that I was deeply conditioned by a society in which the oppressor-victim seesaw is the vehicle for conduct in every area. Now when I find myself targeting a child as responsible for my unhappiness, I realize that I'm feeling victimized by something, perhaps by a situation at work or with a friend, or by my own failure to make time for myself. As soon as I locate the real source of my discomfort, I work to establish balance by inwardly affirming my own value. When we are emotionally isolated from one another we can't even handle simple problems. When we're connected (simply a matter of attitude on my part, usually), we work easily together.

Until I became the mother of school-age sons I thought that sexism worked only against girls. But as soon as my first child entered kindergarten I saw that boys are (I say this deliberately) *equally* oppressed. With the help of my counselor, who works mostly with men, I learned to recognize how boys are systematically coerced into becoming oppressors as a condition of survival, and that they consequently suffer a devastating loss of self.

When my older son entered kindergarten, I asked that he be assigned to the one class that was taught by a man because he had no guiding male presence in his life. Soon after school started my son reported almost casually that on the first day his teacher had hit him in the back with a book. "If I did, and I don't remember doing it, it was only to get his attention," said the teacher when I confronted him. To my lasting shame, I gave this man, who had taught for twenty-five years, another chance. When I visited the classroom before a party or a field trip, I saw no overtly aggressive behavior on the part of the teacher, but I noticed that he always held a group of six or seven little boys apart from the rest of the class and whispered to them intently for a long time.

Later I learned that he was threatening them with punishment if they misbehaved. In February I went to the principal to discuss my concerns; he listened impassively before calling in first the teacher, who explained everything away, and then my son, who could not stick to his stories in the presence of two such intimidating authority figures. He had already learned that truth spoken by a child has no power outside the home, and he feared the consequences of criticizing his teacher. One evening in May, my son suddenly began describing a scene with his teacher on the playground that afternoon. My son was lying on his stomach across the swing. This was not allowed. The teacher called him over, sat him down, and softly said he was very worried about him. If he continued to break little rules, he might start breaking big rules. The teacher said he worked for the School Police ("It's true, Mom, he showed me a card"), and that if my son broke big rules, the School Police would have to come to his house, take him away from his family, and put him in a place where he would learn not to break rules. I took careful notes and read them back to my son to make sure I got everything right. The next morning I called the principal, read him my notes, and told him that my son would not return to school until he was assigned to a different class. My son was moved; he had difficulty settling down; the year ended badly. My son saw me stand up for him, but he saw powerful men make me back down twice before I gained sufficient insight and courage to succeed in protecting him.

Both my children attended the school day care center. My older son is sociable and athletic; his brother is independent and artistic; although they could not be more different, both have bright minds and kind hearts. Both were treated as inherently dangerous and in need of tight controls because they are boys. Their exuberance on the playground gained instant time-outs: "All we were doing was *playing*." If they were hurt they were told that the injury was nothing; if they were frightened they were told not to be silly; if they asked a teacher to solve a conflict they were told to work it out themselves. They were thus instructed quite systematically, if unconsciously, that boys do not suffer pain, do not express fear, and should not look to anyone else for support. If a girl was hurt she was embraced and murmured over; if she was afraid she was reassured warmly; if she complained about mistreatment the culprit was immediately apprehended. Although girls evidently find as much pleasure in annoying other children as boys do (the cruelty of children to each other has shocked me more than anything else I have seen as a parent), no boy is believed when he complains about a girl; no boy is believed when he denies that he bothered a girl.

My younger son always loved costumes and skin painting and ornamentation. Before he started school he went to an in-home day care run by sisters in their early twenties with whom he traded rock music tapes. Sometimes when I picked him up he had bright polish on his tiny stubby fingernails. I learned that all the little kids loved to have their nails painted, but the teachers made sure to remove every trace from every nail of every boy except my son, knowing I enjoyed his fancy fingers and his pleasure in them. The Sunday before the second week of kindergarten I painted my toenails at a friend's house. My son demanded that I do his fingernails too. I wanted him to be free to do what he wanted with his body, but I didn't want him to go to school wearing nail polish. At first I dodged the issue, offering to do his toes, like mine, instead of his fingers. No, he wanted red *finger*nails. "How about clear polish?" offered my friend. *No.* My son was insistent, and baffled by my sudden failure to cooperate. So I had to remind him that everyone out there didn't think the way we did, and that a lot of people had very unfair and rigid ideas about boys and girls, and that one of these was that it was okay for girls to wear makeup but not for boys, and that even though I disagreed I didn't want him to be made fun of, and that was why he should probably wait until next weekend to paint his nails. My son listened patiently and when I was finished he said, "Okay, but I still want to do it now." I groaned helplessly, but my friend said to my son, "Go for it, you've got to face the music some day, and who knows, you might get away with it." I asked, "How will you feel if the kids make fun of you?" "I'll feel bad," he answered, "but I still want to do it." So I painted his nails bright red. A few days later I noticed that he had torn most of the polish off with his teeth. When I asked him why, he answered diffidently, "Joseph said he wouldn't be my friend if I wore nail polish." I knew that Joseph wasn't worthy of his friendship if he cared more about my son's appearance than about his character; that whether he painted his nails or his nose was no one's business but his own. But I also knew that right now he wanted more than anything else for this boy to like him, and that nothing I could say or do would alter his feelings. So I merely explained that this was an example of sexism in action; that his freedom to be *himself* was being limited by other people's ideas about what he was allowed to do *as a boy*, and that I disliked it very much. "I know," he said quietly. As always, for a male child to publicly display interests or behaviors that are considered feminine was to subject himself to ridicule and ostracism. Already largely ignored by the adults at school except when he was perceived as a threat (he was taught from kindergarten on that he was dangerous) and shunned by the girls he had learned to avoid, other boys were his only source of companionship and affirmation, and he could not risk their disapproval. Four years later, his survival instinct and his sense of himself as an individual have merged quite success-fully: he knows, for example, that he can take his origami to school but his knitting stays at home.

I work hard at making my sons participate responsibly in their fam-ily and in society. As soon as they could undress themselves they had to carry their clothes to the laundry basket. As soon as they could feed themselves they had to carry their dishes to the sink. They have to tidy their rooms every other day or so, and they're not allowed to leave their stuff piled on the kitchen table or dropped on the sofa or the floor. They have regular household chores, and they don't get paid for doing them. I do not make a habit of waiting on my children. I want them to under-stand that they are responsible for the space they take up, I want them to know how to maintain their environment, and I don't want them to assume that some woman will always clean up after them. They have to return their phone calls. They have to write thank-you notes. They have to be accountable to themselves and to other people. They can't tell one friend he can spend the night, then decide they'd rather have someone else, and tell the first kid he can't come because they are tired. They can cancel the first friend, but they have to say it's because they're not up to the overnight after all, and they can't then invite the second kid. They have to tell the truth and keep their word.

When I'm feeling optimistic I give myself credit for making them see what I do for them, and for insisting that they respect my need to take care of myself as well. When I'm depressed, I wonder whether they'll grow up thinking that women do everything and men don't do anything they don't want to do. Right now I feel that how I'm doing won't be evi-dent till my boys are fully grown: my success as their parent will be determined by how they treat their lovers and children. In the meantime, there are some things I do consciously to help them become liberated and enlightened men.

I *treat them as equals*. When I was a child I didn't really know the adults who ruled my life. I never saw into their hearts, never knew they grappled with conflicts, never imagined that they had real relationships with each other. I have always lived fully exposed to my kids. From birth they

248

lounged on my lap while I visited with my friends, hearing all the intimate conversations, feeling all our emotions. We have never censored ourselves because children are present. For a long time my kids didn't distinguish between themselves and their friends who happened to be adults. For each of them it was an exotic novelty to have to address adults as "Mr." or "Miss" or, rarely, "Ms." for the first time when they went to school. At home they have always been listened to carefully, included in decision-making whenever possible, and answered honestly and in detail no matter how abstract or personal their questions.

I teach them how to relate to girls and women. I think that the natural narcissism of all children survives as conditioned narcissism in most men. Because my children are boys, I am constantly alert to characteristics that have to be modified if they are to become nonsexist adults. I often see parallels between their behavior toward me and behavior I have resisted in men. For example, a recurring difficulty in my relationships with men has to do with the fact that they don't want me to say no to them. When I say, for example, that I don't want to go to a party, usually the man tries to talk me out of my decision. I stand firm. He argues with me. I stick to my guns. At this point he either becomes angry and attacks my character, or pretends that the discussion never happened and that we are in fact going to the party together (the process may stretch over several days). I have broken off several relationships partly because of the men's inability to accept my right not to do what I don't want to do even if it means disappointing them. My older son often used to run through an identical scenario. Whenever I refused to give him what he wanted, I explained my reasons carefully. He heard me out with unconcealed impatience and then demanded, "But why not?" as though I hadn't said a word. He didn't want to know why at all; he wanted to prolong the argument so he could wear me down and get what he was after. If I eventually lost my temper he would become highly offended, turning a cold shoulder until I caught myself actually apologizing to him for becoming angry. I finally saw that he always managed to turn the focus from his behavior to mine (punishing a woman for expressing anger), putting me on the defensive and pushing the two of us far from the original issue. I was astonished by the extent to which this small child was displaying a manipulative pattern I disliked in grown men. I began to understand that because of the way most men in this culture are treated as children they become terrified when they can't have their own way, as though their very identities are endangered when someone else insists on autonomy. In resisting my son's anxious belligerence, I got the extra strength I needed from my belief that I was teaching him that he can't get what he wants from women by bullying them and that a woman can say no to him and he will survive, their relationship will survive.

When the boys are older I will be unrelenting in my insistence that they be sexually responsible, never leaving protection against pregnancy or disease up to their partner, never accepting a partner's assurance that it's all taken care of.

I teach them about race and class and homophobia. My children know how their food comes to the table and what it costs the Hispanic farm-workers they see in the fields. They notice that most of the janitors they see are black. They respect the homeless almost reverently. They are preoccupied by unfairness. They are tuning their ears to unconscious racism. My sons often ask, "Are we rich?" and, as often, "Are we poor?" Both questions are answered exhaustively. My younger son was born on the third anniversary of two of our oldest friends, a gay couple known with delight as the boys' fairy godfathers. These friends moved from the house where we spent a joyous Thanksgiving because neighboring kids threw rocks in their yard and shouted "Gaylord!" when they went outside; my children were appalled by the news. Their eyes fill with shocked pain when I tell them that the man we met yesterday, so loving and energetic, has AIDS and could not get out of bed today.

I teach them about violence. I think that the rage that leads to violence arises from fear or emotional pain, and I try to stay conscious of how my kids are feeling and attend to their distress at its source. They have never been allowed to hurt each other, and they are shocked by families in which the children's fighting is accepted as normal and inevitable. We do not watch the news on television, but I deliberately expose them to the realities of war and urban and domestic violence. I read to them from the newspaper and cut out pictures that show the torment and devastation that seem so far removed from our apparently safe and genuinely beautiful town. We followed the war in the Persian Gulf in still photographs, from the tanks juxtaposed with camels in the desert to the long lines of surrendering men with their arms held high, begging to be taken. We stared at the image of a young Somali mother waiting by the side of the road for the death cart, her lifeless infant in her arms. Right now on our refrigerator a Bosnian soldier laden with guns nuzzles his baby daughter. We contemplate pictures of gorgeous teenagers in gangs. My boys are irresistibly drawn to blow-'em-up cartoons and explosive movies and comics I can't bear to look at, and I can't claim to understand why. But they easily distinguish between exploitive fiction and the terrible things that happen every minute in actual life, and in the real world they are pacifists. At nine and almost twelve they fear the return of the military draft, and I reassure them firmly that I will not let anyone force them to learn to kill or risk being killed. They know that peace is not a given, at home or in the world, and they willingly open their minds and curb their frustrations and are, I am proud to believe, fundamentally at peace with themselves and each other.

I *teach them to count their blessings*. Children adapt instinctively to the conditions of their lives, no matter how harsh or how luxurious their circumstances may be. They take things for granted. I'm always sticking a metaphorical magnifying glass in front of my kids' faces, keeping up a running commentary on the familiar view before them. As they grow older they become more aware that they are indeed lucky. They live close to nature, with deer in the yard and chickens in the coop and a bluejay who comes into the house and the dull roar and crash of the sea as constant as the mutter and hum of the fridge. They have deep roots in a small community, playing with the children of friends I played with as a child. They are supported in their interests and helped through their difficulties. They eat well and go to sleep unafraid. A big part of my job is to shake them out of their natural complacence, not by threatening them, not by making them feel guilty, but by educating them about the world and getting them to see their place in it now and to imagine the places they'll make for themselves when they grow up.

My older son used to wish I would marry any man who came for dinner more than twice. He accused me of hating men because in explaining why I let them go I sounded critical. In fact, because I have sons I have to make peace in my heart with men. I have to confront my own sexism, and it is humbling to find that it is harder to beat back the thicket of my prejudice than to keep bitter weeds from sprouting in the children's fresher minds. I admire my sons completely. I know their perfection is not my creation, and their presence in my life tests my worth every day. In raising men, I have rescued and am learning to restore myself.

Connie Batten and son Adam.

Winter Solstice

Connie Batten

Outside it was damp and grey. The sun, hidden behind a dense fog bank, was not inviting us to emerge from our tent. We prolonged the inevitable by reading several chapters of a mystery story, huddled in our sleeping bags, tent flap closed against the day. It was Adam's Christmas vacation, and we were spending the first part of it together in a place—on the Northern California coast—that was sacred to me, and at a time of the year—the Winter Solstice—which I have come to hold in reverence.

My son was well aware of my tendency to honor the Winter Solstice in ways that many of his friends would consider rather strange. So I was touched when he willingly agreed to accompany me on this trip out to the land's edge, to one of the points where the continental plates grind and open, where the inner heat of the earth pushes outward and emerges. To make this journey together meant a lot to us both, and both of us made a stretch to meet the other.

We seemed to kind-of know and kind-of not know what day it was, that morning of December twenty-first as we awoke in our tent. This was a special day in another way as well. It was the day when we could move into one of the very precious little cabins on that cliff, overlooking the ocean stretching north toward Stinson Beach. With this incentive we climbed out of the tent, finally, well after daybreak, and, gathering the necessary breakfast things, moved to the protected porch of our cabin for oatmeal and tea and hot chocolate. We savored the flavors slowly, and appreciated the simple comforts we had available to us, as we felt the clouds begin to relinquish their grey hold over the morning.

The sun was high in the sky by the time we began to set forth. We let whim lead us, and we liked where it led. We talked as we climbed, Adam and I, about what makes it hard for us to meet each other sometimes—how he doesn't like some of my preoccupations, like drumming and ceremony and such. And yet how there is some of it that he likes a lot. He talked about what he had enjoyed during our vision quest trip to the desert last summer—the exploring we did, and self-confidence he had gained there.

Back to our cabin in the early afternoon, we put on our wetsuits. And off we went in search of waves to ride. Adam had a boogie board, and I was going to body surf. As I stood, protected by my wetsuit, waiting for a wave to catch, a body-memory began to awaken. It told me just exactly when and where and on which wave to give myself over to the ocean. I knew exactly how to catch a good long ride to shore. As that skill reawakened from my childhood, I experienced it anew—this time with adult awareness. To catch a wave is to relinquish control for a time, allowing the icy water to wash down inside the wet suit, and to surround my uncovered head with aching cold. A mild kind of wildness. And it was quite enough.

After a very arid and head-heavy quarter in graduate school, this ocean-body-mother-son experience was just what I needed to come home to myself, back into my flesh. It was a great blessing. And that wasn't the end. Not at all. There was a minus tide that afternoon which uncovers a hot spring for several hours. When our hands and feet were so frozen that we could no longer feel them, we headed down the cliff to the hot spring. With numb fingers we fumbled out of our wet suits and inched, nude, into the little pools.

I was wary about Adam's sense of well-being, knowing how far this experience was from the steady, linear world he and his father inhabit on the Stanford campus. But he seemed comfortable with it all. I thought, as we sat there, how dreamlike it seemed—in the sense that our excursion represented a visit into the elemental—and how vital it is to maintain a bridge into that world—certainly for me, but also for Adam. These experiences he has with me must have to be relegated to a nearly forgotten part of his psyche during his day-to-day life with his friends and his father. But they are there, and I'm sure they feed him.

And our closeness through that day assures me that there is plenty of positive ambiance available to him from these times we share. I just have to be careful to walk lightly, and let him guide me, when we make those forays into what I call the feminine.

When I think about feminism I am aware that, for me, the concept is not exclusively tied to the imbalances that exist in western culture between men and women. While it is important to me that my children are sensitive to the privilege accorded to boys and men because of their gender, I am also very interested in fostering the reemergence of feminine values in us all, independent of gender. In a world where the masculine values of separateness and independence and dominance have been worshipped for centuries, we have to work hard to rediscover and find time to honor the feminine side of the balance.

Acknowledging the preciousness and fragility and interdependence of our relationships—both with other human beings and with the natural world—is an important aspect of my feminism. It requires me to interrupt my goal-oriented daily life to share these experiences with my children, setting aside time, taking us to places where we have a chance to immerse ourselves in the living universe.

Sitting there in the miracle of warm water for that brief interval in those rocky pools, I was grateful to be able to experience this with Adam, at this particular time, when he is just on the edge of plunging into adolescence.

The day began to wane and we agreed it was time to head back to our new and very temporary, but entirely charming, little home. It was a cabin with no electricity, no running water. I cooked a simple meal, while Adam set about lighting all the candles we could find. We had several feasts—of light and of food—that evening, and settled back into our sleeping bags with more chapters from our mystery book. What better way to lay the solstice to rest.

Biographies

Alta is the founder and publisher of Shameless Hussy Press, America's first feminist press. She is currently producing videos which empower people with disabilities.

Judith Arcana is a writer and teacher. Her most recent book is *Grace Paley's Life Stories, A Literary Biography*. Her son, Dan Arcana, is a photographer and writer who works in theater and film.

Ellen Bass has published several volumes of poetry including *Our Stunning Harvest* from which "Baptism" is taken. She lives in Santa Cruz, California, with her partner, Janet Bryer, and their two children.

Connie Batten is a mother and a grandmother. She is also a woman in midlife, for whom the passage of menopause has been profound. Her work in the world is with conflict resolution. Her work and play at home are about living as simply as possible in close connection with the earth, sky, and changing seasons.

Mary Kay Blakely is the author of *Wake Me When It's Over* and *American Mom* and co-editor of *Pulling Our Own Strings: A Collection of Feminist Humor and Satire*. Her essays have appeared regularly in *The New York Times*, *Vogue*, Ms., and many other journals. She lectures widely and teaches writing at The New School for Social Research.

Claire Braz-Valentine is a widely published poet and playwright. Her three sons, now grown, have successful careers of their own, one as an engineer, one in management, and one as a professional writer.

Maria Bruno is an Associate Professor in the Department of American Thought and Language and Women's Studies at Michigan State University. She is the author of over 30 published short stories and essays and is working on a novel and screenplay.

Naomi Feigelson Chase's most recent book of poetry is *Waiting for the Messiah in Somerville, Mass.* She has also published *The Underground Revolution* (about the sixties), *A Child Is Being Beaten* (about child abuse), and many short stories. She is co-founder of Garden Street Press.

Elayne Clift is a writer and health communication specialist in Potomac, MD. Her latest book is *The Road to Radicalism: Further Reflections of a Frustrated Feminist* (OGN Publications, 1994). Her stories, essays, and poetry have appeared in numerous publications in the U.S. and abroad.

Rachel Clift is a Women's Studies major at Hamilton College in New York. She plans to work with Native American women before going on to graduate school.

Martha Courtot has three daughters and one granddaughter. She is the author of two books, *Tribe* and *Journey*, and has been published in literary and feminist journals and several anthologies. She is currently working on a novel.

Joan Dickenson is a writer, reporter, and columnist who lives in the woods in western New York. Her work has appeared in the anthologies *Shadow on a Tightrope* (Aunt Lute Books) and *Sex Work* (Cleis Press) and in such literary magazines as *Negative Capability*, *Another Chicago Magazine*, and *Blueline*. She was born in 1948.

Susan Eisenberg is a Boston-based writer/artist, union electrician, activist and mother of Zoe and Simon. Acceptance of this essay arrived during Zoe's debut in the Boston Ballet's *Nutcracker* at the Wang Center.

Jean Ellis was educated at the London School of Economics and the School of Oriental and African Studies. From 1976 to 1978 she worked in Cameroon as director of a volunteer program and since then has worked with UK-based voluntary organizations. She and Daniel live in a housing cooperative set up to meet the needs of single-parent families.

Ellen Farmer has spent the last 10 years as a book editor and still manages to write with passion, organizing her mind to meet life's challenges. Lately, she can be found at the health club attempting to organize her other muscles.

Elena Featherston works as a writer, lecturer, and workshop leader, and is the producer/director of the award-winning documentary *Alice Walker: Visions of the Spirit* and editor of *Skin Deep: Women Writing on Color, Cuture, and Identity* (The Crossing Press). She teaches gender and racial equity seminars throughout the U.S. and Europe.

Carol J. Gill is a clinical and research psychologist specializing in disability and identity, including gender issues. Currently, she is conducting a study on disabled women's health experiences at the Chicago Institute of Disability Research. She lives in Darien, IL, with her husband and the family Sheltie.

Joan Joffe Hall has taught English and Women's Studies at the University of Connecticut for years. She has published several volumes of poetry, most recently *Romance and Capitalism at the Movies* (Alice James).

Summer Heat, a collection of stories, was published in 1991. Her son Matthew is now 30.

Laura Hamilton lives in California with her sons Terry and B.J. and her partner, Darcy. She is an educator involved in the interplay of parenting, schooling and the development of social roles for young boys and girls.

Maurice Hamington holds a Ph.D. in Social Ethics and is an Assistant Professor at Mount St. Mary's College in Los Angeles. His primary research interest is Christian feminism. His primary affection interests are Stephanie and Rosemary.

Jeannine Ouellette Howitz writes about mothering and transformation from the center of it. Her work has appeared in *Parents, Ladies' Home Journal, On the Issues*, and other magazines. *Magic Moons*, her first picture book for children, is forthcoming from Orchard Books.

Katherine Keefer is a sculptor who lives and works in Oakland, California. "Raising Aaron" was written at the suggestion of a friend. Currently a collection of her letters is being put into manuscript form.

Lucy Kemnitzer is 40, married, with a teenaged son and a daughter beginning grade school. She has worked in various industries and been active in labor and community struggles. A teacher and writer of fiction, she also writes a column on childrearing and social issues for a women's newspaper.

Marilyn Krysl is the author of five books of poetry and numerous essays, articles, and reviews published in *The Atlantic, The Nation, The New Republic* and many other journals, as well as in O. *Henry Prize Stories* and the *Pushcart Prize Anthology*. She was awarded the University of Colorado Faculty Book Prize for *Mozart, Westmoreland and Me*.

Adair Lara is a staff columnist for *The San Francisco Chronicle* and the author of *History of Petaluma: A California River Town* (Scottwall Associates, 1982), *Welcome to Earth, Mom* (Chronicle Books, 1992), and *Slowing Down in a Speeded-Up World* (Conari, 1994). Her work also appears in several magazines.

Li Min Hua is the author of over one thousand published works, including *Sunspots, Midnight Lessons*. Li professes English at Rutgers, The State University of New Jersey.

Audre Lorde, poet, novelist, essayist, educator and activist, died of cancer in November, 1992. She is the author of ten volumes of poetry, a novel, and numerous essays which have been widely reprinted and translated. Her last book, published after her death, is *The Marvelous Arithmetics of Distance*.

Kate Luna writes and performs autobiographical stories for stage and live radio. "Boy Thangs" is adapted from her show, *True Kid*. She combines mothering her 12-year-old son with her work as a writer, storyteller, and visual artist from their home in the remote hills of Cazadero, California.

Anne Mackenzie is a writer, mother, and half owner of a small publishing company. Tyler Mackenzie-Elkins is presently 12 years old. They share a house and life with Anne's sister and niece, as well as three cats, one dog, two birds, one rat, one chameleon, and one goldfish that refuses to die.

Carolina Mancuso has had fiction published in *Ikon and Amelia*, and in the anthologies *Love, Struggle & Change*, *Word of Mouth* 1 and 2 (Crossing), and *How To* (Violet Ink). One of her stories received the Reed Smith Fiction Award and was nominated for the Pushcart Prize. She teaches at New York University where she is working on her doctoral dissertation.

G. Marault lives in Minnesota.

Kathleen Melin is a mother, writer and wife. She finds it hard to seem conventional in politically charged times. Her two sons, one daughter, and partner are the essence of her education. She is also an M.A. student in Creative Writing at the University of Minnesota.

Barbara Miller resides in Eugene, OR, where she is serving her tour de force as the mom of her three teenage sons. She figures that her greatest achievement as a feminist parent, to date, is that her oldest son's girlfriend is a feminist! Barbara works as an educator for teen moms and other at-risk adolescents.

E.L. Moore is a recent graduate of Oberlin College, where she majored in Women's Studies, edited a progressive Jewish student newspaper, lobbied for a campus sexual harassment policy, and learned the art of activism. She currently works as a secretary in San Francisco.

Robin Morgan, poet, political theorist, activist, and writer, is editor-in-chief of *Ms.* magazine. Her books include *Sisterhood is Powerful*, *Sisterhood is Global*, *Going Too Far*, *The Anatomy of Freedom*, *The Demon Lover*, the novel *Dry Your Smile*, and five volumes of poetry. She lives in New York City.

Rochelle Natt has published in many literary magazines and anthologies. In 1993 she was a finalist in the Eve of St. Agnes short story competition and the Judah Magdes Award for a poem on the Jewish experience. Her daughter, Heather, is a freshman at Columbia University.

Ní Aódagaín is a 37-year-old white lesbian mother, writer, and editor, who writes of the rewarding, challenging, demanding and often invisible work of raising a child, especially as a feminist. She hopes her words give strength to other women who are doing this vital work of raising the next generation.

Robyn Parnell, who really doesn't think Barry is such an awful name, lives and writes (or tries to write, since the birth of her son, Eli) in Hillsboro, Oregon.

Penny Perkins is a writer and editor living in Hoboken, N.J. She has been published in *Queer City: The Portable Lower East Side* and *Girlfriend Number One*. She has finished a collection of short stories and is currently working on a novel.

Letty Cottin Pogrebin is the author of seven books including *Growing Up Free, Family Politics*, and most recently, *Deborah, Golda, and Me: Being Female and Jewish in America*. She is a founding editor and now contributing editor of *Ms.* magazine. She is married and the mother of three adult children.

Shirley Powers is the author of *With No Slow Dance* (Two Steps In Press, 1980). Her work has also appeared in *Matrix, Earth's Daughters, Iris, Iowa Woman*, and *Different Daughters: A Book By Mothers of Lesbians*.

Minnie Bruce Pratt is the mother of two sons and the author of *Crime Against Nature* (Firebrand Books), a book about their relationship, which was chosen as the 1989 Lamont Poetry Selection by the Academy of American Poets. She currently lives in Jersey City, NJ, and is working on *S/he*, a volume of prose poems about crossing gender boundaries.

Anna Quindlen is a Pulitzer Prize-winning *New York Times* columnist and the author of *Living Out Loud, Object Lessons*, and a children's book, *The Tree That Came to Stay*. In 1988 she was named one of the outstanding mothers in America by the National Mother's Day Committee.

Gail S. Rebhan's photographs are in the following collections: National Museum of American Art, Corcoran Gallery of Art, Getty Museum and Polaroid Corporation. She has exhibited in Germany and England as well as the U.S., and is an Assistant Professor at Mount Vernon College in Washington, D.C.

Victoria Alegria Rosales, a recent M.F.A. graduate, is looking for a teaching job. Her specialty is poetry, fiction and magic realism. *Nopales for My Ancestors* is her forthcoming book of poetry.

Sally Rosloff, born in 1949, lives in southern California with her husband, two children and cat. She is currently a project manager in the Department of University Relations at UCLA. Active in the women's movement in the early '80s, her interests now include parenting, education reform and health/nutrition issues.

Lynn Saul is a lawyer, poet, and teacher. In the '70s, when her children were growing up, she was a legal activist for women. In 1982 she moved to the Tohono O'Odham reservation and her children lived with their father. She now practices law in Tucson, teaches writing at Pima College and civil rights law at the University of Arizona.

Ardena Shankar is mother to adult twin daughters and grandmother to three boys and one girl. She is a writer, poet, and consultant who lives in Santa Cruz, CA, where she facilitates workshops for the empowerment of women.

Deborah Shouse's current koan is "A clear mind—what is it?" She has a petite book of fiction, *White Bread Love*, and writing that appears in *Christian Science Monitor*, *Tampa Tribune*, *The Sun*, and the anthology *The Time of Our Lives*.

Penelope Sky and her sons are natives of redwood canyons and bare ridges above the sea. They work hard but they are very lucky: they live with lots of animals and have many good friends. They worry about the state of the world, yet manage to enjoy themselves and each other enormously.

Do Mi Stauber is a freelance indexer, artist, singer and parent who lives in Eugene, OR. She and her partner work together training preschool and elementary teachers in antibias, diversity-affirming education, and hope to start a newsletter for parents on nonsexist childraising.

Judith Wolinsky Steinbergh has published four books of poetry (most recently A *Living Anytime* (Talking Stone Press) and co-authored *Beyond Words, Writing Poems with Children*. A Poet-in-the-Schools since 1970 and a Wordswork Prize for poetry winner, her stories and poems appear in *Calyx*, *Sojourner*, *The Worcester Review*, and other journals.

Becky Taylor is a Computer Science student at the University of California, Santa Cruz. Her writing has appeared in *Woman of Power*.

Dena Taylor is the author of *Red Flower: Rethinking Menstruation* and the co-editor of three anthologies on women's issues. She lives in California, works in publishing, and teaches Women's Studies at Cabrillo College.

Jean Tepperman is a freelance writer living on the San Francisco peninsula.

Gail Thomas is the single, lesbian parent of two daughters, 15 and 17. She is a teacher and poet whose work has been published in a variety of small magazines and journals.

Suzanne Tingley is a school superintendent in upstate New York. She is a writer on educational issues, and her essays have appeared in numerous national educational publications.

Barbara Unger has published in *The Nation*, *The Literary Review*, *The Massachusetts Review*, *Southern Humanities Review* and many anthologies.

Alma Luz Villanueva is the author of *The Ultraviolet Sky*, which won an American Book Award, *Naked Ladies*, *Weeping Woman: La Llorona and Other Stories* (novels and short stories), and six books of poetry, most recently *Planet*.

Larry A. Voss is an educator and researcher studying ways to integrate children with disabilities into mainstream education while preserving their self-esteem and pride in the disability culture. He served as Faculty Chair of the West Valley Special Education Center in Los Angeles and currently is Executive Director of the Chicago Institute of Disability Research.

Roz Warren is a happily married radical feminist mom, and the editor of *Women's Glib*, *Women's Glibber*, *Mothers!*, *What Is This Thing Called Sex?*, *Kitty Libber: Cat Cartoons by Women* and *Glibquips*, all published by The Crossing Press.

Trisha Whitney is living her dream in Eugene, OR, teaching in her own alternative school, the Drinking Gourd Elementary School, and raising a wonderful daughter.

Maureen Williams is a writer, editor and publisher transplanted from Britain over 13 years ago, now living in the forested mountains of Pennsylvania. Her quarterly magazine, *Keltic Fringe*, provides news and features on all aspects of Keltic life and history.

Suggested Reading

Beginning Equal: A manual about nonsexist childrearing for infants and toddlers, by the Project BE staff. Women's Action Alliance, New York, 1983.

Daughters of Feminists: Young Women with Feminist Mothers Talk About Their Lives by Rose Glickman. St. Martin's Press, 1993.

Different Mothers by Louise Rafkin. Cleis Press, 1990

Equal Their Chances: Children's Activities for Non-Sexist Learning by June Shapiro, Sylvia Kramer and Catherine Hunerberg. Prentice-Hall, 1981.

Every Mother's Son by Judith Arcana. The Women's Press, London, 1992.

Growing Up Free by Letty Cottin Pogrebin. McGraw-Hill, 1980.

Lives Together/Worlds Apart: Mothers and Daughters in Popular Culture by Suzanna Walters. University of California Press, 1992.

Meeting at the Crossroads by Lyn Mikel Brown and Carol Gilligan. Ballantine Books, 1992.

Mother Daughter Revolution by Elizabeth Debold, Marie Wilson and Idelisse Malave. Addison-Wesley, 1993.

Non-Sexist Childraising by Carrie Carmichael. Beacon Press, 1977.

Non-Sexist Education for Young Children by Barbara Sprung. Citation Press, 1975.

Of Woman Born by Adrienne Rich. W.W. Norton & Co., 1976.

*The Crossing Press
publishes many
titles of interest
to women.
For a free catalog,
call toll-free*
800-777-1048.